# YouTube

*Ultimate YouTube Guide to Building a Channel, Audience, and to Start Making Passive Income*

**Andrew Mckinnon**

*Andrew Mckinnon*

Disclaimer Notice:

Please note the information contained within this document is for educational and entertainment purposes only. Every attempt has been made to provide accurate, up to date and reliable complete information. No warranties of any kind are expressed or implied. Readers acknowledge that the author is not engaging in the rendering of legal, financial, medical or professional advice.

# Table of Contents

# Introduction

The Internet is here to stay. I know it, you know it, and so does everybody else. Ever since the digital age began, everything somehow seems to be connected to the Internet in one way or the other. And things without an online presence seem to have an unsustainable future.

There was a time when people had little to no access to the Internet, and yet it managed to impact their lives in some way or the other. But once it came along, there was no stopping it from affecting people's lives in a big way. People were skeptical about it at first but slowly began to embrace it and took pride in using the Internet. Their lives became easier, and they were able to do more in a short period of time. The Internet slowly became an important part of everybody's life, and they began to be extra productive.

Right from housewives to students to working professionals, everybody began to use the Internet to gather information, access data, upload, download, etc. All this made their lives easier, and they found themselves doing more work in a shorter timeframe. Businesses, too, started to use the Internet as a way to communicate with customers, keep in touch with traders, and used it for many other business related purposes. This helped them avail a larger audience and do more things on a daily basis. Business entities had to get word of their business out there in order to attract more and more customers.

It is obvious that every business has one goal in mind, and that is to earn the maximum amount of profit that they possibly can. Various different methods can be used to achieve this, and a constant effort needs to be made to keep up with the latest developments for said purpose.

Now putting both profit and the Internet together, you can probably make out that this book has to do with something related to them. And what we are going to discuss is how you can earn a lot of money from an online business. More specifically, you will learn how to make money from your own YouTube channel.

Most of you are already familiar with the YouTube website which is a popular social media platform for sharing videos. How many times have you watched a show or seen a movie on it? I'm sure by now you have also toyed with the idea of signing up and uploading your own videos on the site because that is what YouTube is all about. It is all about "you". The site is the most-visited video site in the world and has garnered popularity owing to its ease of access and use. Every day, millions of people access it to watch their favorite videos and entertain themselves. Everything from funny videos to horror to music videos, the site is full of videos that are uploaded from around the world and also has videos in possibly every language. The best part is, it is all for free. So, as long as you have an Internet connection, you will have the chance to watch a video and seek entertainment. You will be able to watch videos and movies of your choice, and you can do it the entire day. There is also the live version on the site, which plays live videos that are streamed from the live venues.

The site provides people with ample entertainment, no doubt, but there is a lot of scope to turn your channel into a money-earner. Yes, that's right. You can use your YouTube channel to draw in large crowds and use it to your advantage.

What we are going to talk about is how this website can be used not just for entertainment but also as a source of earning some money. Since the platform is online, the audience you can generate is huge. and so the chances of you earning some good money are also pretty good. You will be surprised to see how easy it is for you to set up a line of passive income and all you have to do is spend a little time in front of your computer.

By the time you are done reading this book, you will know exactly where to go and what to do in order to start making money with your Internet account. You cannot lead a life anymore if you are not present on the Internet, and this book will surely help you establish a successful business on the Internet.

Use the information and guidelines given here to create your own successful YouTube channel!

Let us start.

# Chapter 1

# About YouTube

As we have mentioned above, most of you are already familiar with YouTube. And for the rest of you, this chapter should give you a head start in learning more about it.

As was mentioned earlier, the Internet started to make a big impact in the 90s. Better known as the dot com bubble, there were a lot of websites that started to crop up, and more and more people began to fancy the web. They wanted to learn about it and use it to their advantage. Out of these people, there were those who jumped at the opportunity of understanding what the Internet is really about and began to profit out of it. They are now millionaires, owing to the hard work that they put in, and were amply rewarded for recognizing the Internet's true potential.

Right from trading stocks to writing on important topics, it was suddenly possible for people to do much more than what they could before. From sharing pictures to videos, it was all doable within the click of a button. That is when people began to research the things that can be done on the Internet. They started uploading data and understood just how many use it worldwide. There were some who understood that videos were being watched and that it has a big market. More and more people wanted to watch videos, as it is better than having to read something. That is probably what prompted the creators of YouTube to start a website that played videos.

The YouTube video-sharing website was started as an independent company in 2005 by Chad Hurley, Jawed Karim, and Steve Chen, all of whom used to previously work at PayPal. The main office is in San Bruno, California, and in 2006, Google acquired it.

The first video was uploaded by Jawed, who taped himself at the zoo, and it went viral. More and more people realized that they could upload and watch whatever they liked and use the site to their advantage. It set in motion a culture that started gaining in strength. Today, YouTube has hundreds of thousands of hours of videos available for people to watch. This means that there has been a revolution of sorts, and one video is played every second around the world. The site is available for access in every corner of the planet. As long as there is an Internet access, there is YouTube.

It was important to create an account earlier to watch some of the videos that were not suited for all audiences, but when Google took over, people had the convenience of logging in from their Google accounts and didn't have to create a separate account on YouTube. This move made them even more accessible, so more and more people started to discover the benefits of having a website that plays all sorts of videos from the world over.

People can use this site for watching, uploading, or sharing any videos deemed appropriate on the website. The videos can be short clips, blogger content, music videos, or even movies. The scope of how many different things can be conveyed through this social media is vast and has seen an ever-growing audience since its release.

The user who uploads the content could be anyone. You can start your own channel on this website like thousands of other individuals. All you have to do is register on the site, and it's absolutely free! You will also notice that many companies like Vevo have their own channel on YouTube since they can reach out to far more people online. There are also record companies, artists, and other such big names that utilize YouTube to reach the masses. Not only is it free for all, but the range of audiences they reach is simply superb. I'm sure you are aware of Justin Beiber and how he used YouTube to turn popular. Similarly, there are several people out there who use it as a platform to get noticed and make it big. So, it is completely up to you to choose what you wish to do with YouTube, and there are absolutely no restrictions to what you can and cannot do with it. As long as it complies with the basic requirements, you can upload your videos and reach a wide audience.

The developers of this website have utilized the scope of social media to their maximum benefit and made it as user friendly as they possibly could. The design of the website has been improved continuously over the years to make it simple to understand and used by the layman. Hence, the audience of this website is said to be way more than any television channel on a daily basis.

Any YouTube user can upload videos on the website after registering. The site has some rules about uploading unauthorized content and has tried to prevent it through these rules. It was observed that most videos, which had unauthorized uploads of movies, series, etc., were quite long in duration. To prevent this, the site allows users only 15-minute videos to be uploaded when they start out on the forum. Over time, if the site feels that the user is trustworthy, they are permitted more time. Verification of the user's account via mobile phone also increases the chances of their being able to upload longer videos on YouTube. This is necessary if you are trying to upload a documentary you shot or upload a nice movie that will invite a lot of viewers. Remember, your content will ultimately determine who watches your videos and how many people you can attract. So, you have to try and earn the right to upload lengthier videos if you wish to make it big with YouTube.

Video formats which are supported on YouTube include .AVI, .MPEG, .WMV, .OGV, .MPS, .MKV, .FLV, .VO

B, etc. Any videos uploaded on the site should be in these formats for the site to accept it.

Another great feature of YouTube is that a user can upload the content from there to other websites. The URL for the video just needs to be embedded on the other site, and any audience there can view it. This further helps in increasing the accessibility to the videos on this platform.

Although the videos uploaded on this website cannot be downloaded directly, many third-party websites have enabled the user to do so. However, the YouTube website itself intends that all users view the video as content on their site itself.

Yet another plus point is that the website can be viewed on many different platforms varying from mobile phones, tablets, laptops, etc. The site even launched an application that optimized the viewing of their content on mobile devices. It is easily accessible by users all over the world who can use such devices. Also, the interface is available in 61 different languages to make it accessible to as many people as possible. So, all you need is a device and an Internet connection to play your videos and enjoy them. As of June 2015, YouTube has also introduced the brand new feature of downloading videos and watching them even without an active Internet connection. This is a big boon to all those who wish to watch videos but don't have Internet access like while travelling or going to places where Internet is not available.

Over the years, the YouTube platform has established itself at an amazing rate. People have used it for a variety of different things, which are not just about providing viewers with entertainment. Many different social causes have been promoted and thus aided with the use of this website. The large worldwide audience gives a larger scope for reaching out to more people and making a bigger difference in the world. Even people without televisions can access all the important video content in the world on this website. This has helped in increasing social awareness on different fronts. This popularity is said to grow owing to the rate at which YouTube has grown within a span of 10 years. There is just so much to do and it still feels like we are in the initial stages of a bigger revolution. Through support and encouragement received from all fronts, YouTube is slowly moving towards becoming one of the largest and most popular entities on the Internet. It is taking many people and projects under its wings and soaring high.

We now know that the YouTube website has gained an extremely huge following since its release, and it just seems to be growing over time, and that this is a great opportunity for you to use the site to your advantage. When it started out, people didn't think far enough, but as it became obvious that the site had huge potential for generating income from all the audience, people started finding ways to earn money from it as well. And here we will tell you how you can do this too.

The investment required with starting your own YouTube channel is nil, and so there's more to invest in other aspects of the online source of income you want to develop. Doesn't this sound like the most perfect plan to start something useful - to not invest any money initially and make the most of this ideal situation?

Google uses a program called Google AdSense, which is used to advertise and generate revenue on the website. Using their AdWords and AdSense programs is a simple way to earn cash on YouTube.

There are many other ways in which you can utilize this popular social platform for business. As you read on, you will get a step-by-step guide on how to create your own YouTube channel. You will then see exactly how to use YouTube for marketing and other business purposes. Once you are through, you can easily generate an income using YouTube. But for that, you need to first understand the concept clearly and then move on to the earning money bit; you cannot rush into something without thinking it through.

*Andrew Mckinnon*

# Chapter 2

# Features and Impact of YouTube

There are several features of YouTube that makes it a suitable platform for video hosting, video watching, and video browsing. Some of the features are listed below:

## Playback

When YouTube was initially founded, it required a plug-in called the Adobe Flash Player installed in the browser for viewing on computers. However, in the year 2010, a Beta version of YouTube was created that supported and used the HTML5 standard that was supported by several web browsers due to their multimedia capabilities. This enabled users to watch videos without the Adobe Flash Player plug-in to be installed. The users could now use this new feature and opt for the HTML5 trial. The problem with the Beta version was that only some videos were available. Also, only those web browsers that supported HTML5 using WebM format and H.264 formats could play the videos. In the year 2015, HTML5 became the default playback method for all browsers like Internet Explorer 11, Google Chrome, and Safari 8. An adaptive HTTP-based streaming solution was adapted, which helped to control the quality of videos, and the bit rate of the videos on YouTube through the Dynamic Adaptive Streaming over HTTP. With this success, they are now supported by the Adobe Dynamic Streaming for Flash.

## Uploading

When YouTube was initially launched, it was possible upload long videos. However, the team at YouTube found that the long videos had copyrighted content and unauthorized TV programs, serials, and movies. Hence, in March 2006, an upper limit of ten minutes was introduced. This limit increased to 15 minutes in the year 2010, and today all users can upload videos up to 15 minutes. YouTube has a feature wherein those users who comply with the Community Guidelines can upload videos of up to 12 hours. This requires account verification along with a cell phone. Videos on YouTube can be uploaded in various formats and almost all formats are accepted by YouTube including .MOV, .DivX, .OGG, .AVI, .MKV, .OGY, .VOB, .M PEG, .WMV, .MP4, and .MPEG-4. YouTube has also enabled mobile uploads using the 3GP format. The video formats use progressive scanning and are only then uploaded on YouTube. Those with interlaced scanning are required to be changed into a progressive scanning format as it reduces the clarity of the video.

## Quality and Formats

When it first came out, YouTube offered all its videos only with the mono MP3 audio and used the Sorenson Spark codec. This was similar to H.263, and the videos had a resolution of 320×240 pixels. This was extended to a higher resolution of 480×360 pixels in 2008. YouTube also offered the option of watching videos on phones using the 3GP format. It has progressively increased the amount of resolution for watching videos; for instance, in the year 2008, videos could be streamed at a resolution of 720 pixels in high definition. During this time, the player size was increased to a ratio of 16:9 widescreen as opposed to the previous 4:3 aspect. YouTube also changed its default video compressing format to H.264/MPEG-4 AVC. The next year, that is, 2009, it supported 1080 pixel worth of resolution in high definition. In 2010, the 4K format was introduced, which supported videos with a resolution of up to 4096×3072 pixels. In 2015, YouTube increased its support base to 8K-resolution format, and videos could be played at 7680×4320 pixels. Videos are also offered in various qualities including standard quality (SQ), high quality (HQ), and high definition (HD). These are represented by the resolution and pixels.

## Content Accessibility

YouTube is one of the few video streaming and uploading websites that makes their videos accessible from other web pages. They have a HTML link that is usually below the video that enables sharing. This has spurted the increase in the amount of videos shared on social networking platforms like Facebook and various blogs. In the year 2013, YouTube removed its video response feature that previously allowed users to respond to videos. This was due to the lack of response and use. It is user friendly in a way such that it allows disabling and enabling of comments, ratings, posting of responses, and embedding. Only a few videos can be directly downloaded, like the presidential addresses or weekly reports. These can usually be downloaded as a MP4 file. However, conventionally speaking, it does not allow the download of videos directly. All videos can only be viewed through the interface of its website. With the popularity of videos and the demands of the people for video downloads, several websites, plug-ins, and applications have made downloads of videos easy. A service test was conducted in the year 2009 to allow video downloads for free. There were also test services conducted for download through the payment of a small fee using Google Checkout. With more sites making the download of illegal videos easy, YouTube threatened legal action against several video-downloading platforms to remove their feature enabling downloads from YouTube. However, if videos do not have any copyrighted material, then it is possible to reuse and remake the material without facing adverse consequences.

## Platforms

YouTube videos can be viewed through most smart phones and tablets. This can be done by installing the YouTube application for the particular phone or using an optimized browsing page. In the year 2007, using RTSP streaming, YouTube mobile was launched. However, it must be noted that not all videos are viewable on smart phones. Apple enabled YouTube videos on several of its products and this is done by converting the standard YouTube content's transcript and transcode into Apple's default settings of H.264. Today, the videos can be accessed from the iPhone, the Apple TV, iPod Touch, and so on. Due to the complications faced by the mobile version of YouTube, in 2010, YouTube came up with a relaunch of the mobile version. This version operated on HTML5 instead of the Adobe Flash Player. Videos were navigated and controlled using touch screen set up. Android released the YouTube app to enable video watching and video upload.

The YouTube app was initially started in 2012, and it was commemorated by being launched for the iPhone. Apple soon made the YouTube app one of the preloaded apps that came with the iPhone, since the advent of the iOS 6 operating system and the iPhone 5. According to several surveys and data sources, the YouTube app is one of the most widely used apps with about 35 percent of smart phone users using it. In fact, as of 2013, it is the third most widely used app. In 2008, the TiVo service came up enabling the search and play of YouTube videos in the system. It also came up with YouTube for TV, which was customized in accordance to the set top boxes and media devices that had web browsers like Wii video game consoles and PlayStation 3. This was extended in 2009 when YouTube came up with the YouTube XL, which allowed the YouTube web page to be displayed on a standard television screen using a simpler design interface. The YouTube app is also compatible with the XBox Live, and official apps customized for Wii were also created in 2012. This allowed users to watch several videos from the Wii channel. Other such compatible devices include the Wii U and Nintendo 3DS. It is also available on the Roku Player as of 2013. The Wii U Internet Browser uses HTML 5, which is the default code for YouTube; hence videos can be watched and browsed on Wii U. Sony PlayStation 4 has also been compatible with YouTube as of 2014.

## Localization

In 2007, the CEO of Google launched the new localization system in Paris. The localized version of YouTube was released in about 79 countries in a standard version worldwide. This used the IP address of the user to switch to the localized version. The YouTube interface identified the territory in which the user was located and customized his or her video viewing experience based on that territory. This is why, in some cases, videos weren't available for all countries. The message, "This video is not available in your country" was displayed on videos with inappropriate content or copyrighted content. About 76 language versions of YouTube are allowed in the interface of the website. Some of them are Bengali, Kazakh, Urdu, Azerbaijani, Laotian, and Burmese; these do not have local channel versions. Several nations blocked YouTube. For instance, Turkey blocked YouTube from 2008 until 2010, and this was attributed to video postings with offensive material. In 2012, this ban was lifted and a localized version of YouTube was set up under the domain of youtube.com.tr. This was controlled by the Turkish government, and all content was allowed only with the consent and permission of Turkish law. Disputes have also been a common event. In 2009, the British Royalty Agency called PRS for Music about a dispute with YouTube. Music videos were blocked from being accessible to the British population. This came about due to the disagreement in the licensing of major record companies. This was solved in the same year. A similar incident happened to the population of Germany.

## Education and Knowledge

According to the curator of TED talks, Chris Anderson, it is possible for the human brain to decode videos. Breaking down videos is easier than breaking down written information or any other form of communication. YouTube revolutionized face-to-face communication, and the fine-tuning of it has made YouTube on par with Gutenberg. Now, YouTube has increased efficiency even more than Gutenberg. This also increased development in science and technology and became a platform for knowledge and learning.

One of the greatest examples of how YouTube revolutionized learning is through the Khan Academy. Salman Khan founded the Khan Academy to teach his cousin. YouTube tutorials were created on various subjects, and soon this became the largest school in the world. With about ten million students, 26,000 videos with 370 million views, YouTube was a mark of how people progressed. It broke down the traditional barriers of learning with decreased costs, uniform content, and reached once inaccessible pockets of the world. Students could now work at their own speed and pace without disrupting their schedule. It resulted in the coming up of technology-forward people who embraced this new knowledge platform. Today, colleges, universities, schools, and other educational institutions make extensive use of YouTube videos to train and develop both teachers and students to create better understanding of their subjects.

## Searchable Information

Forrester Research classified YouTube as the largest video platform. In the year 2012, it also happened to be the world's second largest search engine with the only drawback being that search keywords were limited to the video titles, labels, and tags, as opposed to the content of the videos.

## Innovation Through Distributed Channels

After YouTube was launched in 2005, the earliest content creators and video uploaders gained massive amounts of views and hits. Their videos had larger viewing audiences, and hence several of them created communities among their video viewers. Chris Anderson stated that people from various areas brought their skills together. These skills were shared, leading to development and challenging people of other geographical locations to develop their skills. This increased innovation and invention. YouTube linked the global world together. For instance, producers of dance companies have noticed that students from America took videos of dance lessons from Japanese dance companies and remade them to suit their style, while Japanese students remixed several American videos to suit their needs. New dance styles, music styles, and new types of cinematography have caused an evolution in videography that is attributed to the global linkage that YouTube provides. Covers and remakes of music videos have served as inspiration to several people, and soon the site became a harbinger of influence, inspiration, and imitation. In fact, a cover by a guitarist received millions of videos and this led to several users creating covers imitating *him*.

Journalists have found a pattern here; YouTube is not only a platform for watching and hosting videos, but it also became a phenomenon by changing cultures, breaking barriers, and influencing future generations. With this came an influx of inventors. It also provided a platform for scientists, inventors, and researchers to test their theories and concepts. With YouTube, it was easier to collaborate and get answers.

Google purchased YouTube, and after its purchase, several companies started to dominate the channels. This increased the target audience and revolutionized cultural expression. They were able to receive more hits on their channels, leading to an increase in marketing reach. They also encountered more customer satisfaction and could make their products tailor-made to their customers.

## Collaboration and Crowdsourcing

YouTube also served as a way through which people could recognize and form groups and squads. For instance, several projects made use of the video website to assemble people from across the globe to celebrate events. One such prominent case was that of the YouTube Symphony Orchestra which made use of the video website to host auditions. Individuals and musicians were selected based on their performance. This linked people from different towns and failed to discriminate among the various cities and villages. Suddenly, people living in remote locations had the same chance and opportunity as those who were living in larger cities. Mergers were also made wherein people from various locations collaborated to create videos without meeting each other. This broke the geographical barriers of location and time difference. Crowdsourced videos gained massive popularity leading to a large amount of donations. Several non-governmental organizations, charity organizations, and advocates of social welfare created channels to increase their donations. In fact, Lisa Lavie's 57-contributor charity came up with the collaborative video performed by several artists, "We are the World 25 for Haiti." This was done to raise money for the victims of the 2010 Haiti earthquake. Similarly, other charity channels collaborated for giving aid and raising funds for tsunami victims and hurricane victims, among others. "Life in a Day" was a full length YouTube-partnered documentary, which was a collaborative effort of several people, that was the first crowd-sourced movie, released in 2011. It featured 80,000 submitted videos from video uploaders and featured scenes and footage from the life of the video uploaders.

## Broadening Awareness of Social Issues

Awareness programs on social issues and help lines were created, leading to more widespread knowledge. Projects like the "It Gets Better" project served as an anti-bullying campaign, which gained massive attention after its launch on YouTube. The project aimed at targeting suicidal LGBT teenagers and discouraging the stigma associated with them. Within a few weeks of its launch, several responses came about from users and celebrities expressing their concern and support. The project gained so much attention that the US President Barack Obama, cabinet secretaries, diplomats, officials, and staff of the government responded positively to this project.

YouTube music videos in support of several causes were also launched. Videos and documentaries relating to the life of people who dealt with bullying, abuse, and other social stigmas were also released. One such was Amanda Todd's video which was titled "My Story: Struggling, Bullying, Suicide, Self-Harm." This was posted a month before her suicide, causing such problems to take the limelight. Media coverage became controversial in this aspect because psychologists believed that the hype and sensationalization of the story would inspire more suicide for the attention. This inspired anti-bullying campaigns, and strategies after bullying were studied and researched in detail.

Many YouTube personalities also used the platform for other good causes. Celebrities and prominent YouTube users used the website to raise money for problems. One such was the Trevor Project that was supported by Tyler Oakley, which raised thousands of dollars for the cause. The Trevor Project advocated the rights of LGBTQ youth and aimed at preventing their abuse and suicide.

## Effects on Values and Standards

Entertainment Weekly's "100 Greatest" was a list that featured YouTube in 2009. According to the team there, YouTube was a home for cat videos, cooking shows, celebrity goof ups, and music covers since its inception in 2005. Charlie Bit My Finger was the most watched video as of 2010 and this threw light on the content quality of the videos. Many people in the entertainment industry stated that YouTube had changed the conventional norms of quality. This video served as an example of how the masses responded to video, regardless of the content. The influx of advertising agents and journalists also enhanced the video content on YouTube. The site redefined videos and quality. Several researchers credited the acceptance of low-quality videos, and even ones without mainstream content, to the low expectations of the masses. The lack of professionally made videos did not deter viewers.

## Journalism

YouTube also helped to recreate and redefine journalism. The students and researchers of A Pew Research Center studied the effects of YouTube in terms of journalism, and their studies concluded that YouTube had created a new branch of journalism called the video journalism. In this form, eyewitnesses, citizens, and established organizations helped to create content. The most-watched videos were in current affairs or news. Responses and views of the news articles also flooded the scene. This increased flow of information and development of ideas and strategies. YouTube served as a catalyst to increase the response and channel the thinking of the population. News channels also created videos for YouTube propagating and advocating certain news articles that could impact the crowd, and often these channels had more views than the conventional TV views. YouTube also came up with live streaming. The 2012 Summer Olympic Games were covered live on YouTube. Similarly, the site also streamed the speeches of the important political parties during the elections.

It was also particularly useful to bridge gaps in communication. For instance, many news channels could get an idea of the views of the people through comments, ratings, and video responses, which are not something that could be done with conventional forms of journalism.

## Direct Effect on World Events

YouTube has been a positive force a well as a catalyst in formulating opinion for the people. One of the videos, "Innocence of Muslims," which was a YouTube video produced in the year 2012, was made by a user in United States, and this was circulated among audiences leading to protests. Several Muslims protested vehemently and believed the entire video to be a mockery of Muhammad.

This gained worldwide attention as anti-American violence began to spread, even though the US Government did not advocate the video.

Similarly, a video that showed Neda Agha-Soltan's death gained massive popularity in the positive way. It was captured on a mobile phone camera and depicted the death of an Iranian student during the Iranian election protests in 2009. This gained the George Polk Award in journalism. It became a video that was as important as the news itself. The award meant the acknowledgement of a regular citizen in politics and the role the public played in showing information that could be withheld by journalists. This video also served as a symbol for the opposition movement to the Iranian government.

There were also several videos that triggered issues like the one made by Anwar al-Awlaki. He was an al-Qaeda militant who encouraged attacks against the United States. These videos were eventually removed by the team at YouTube, though in the initial stages, they triggered and inspired violent attacks on Americans. Mockeries, parodies, and documentaries that impacted the public in a bad light were usually removed. One such video was the sentencing of eight video uploaders who uploaded a video that showed the Gangsta culture of teens in the UAE. The video showed mild forms of violence that the court believed showed the UAE in a bad light; this lead to several laws being enacted - one such law being the cyber crime law that stated that severe action would be taken if any act was done to endanger the state. This lead to protests and criticisms, citing right to freedom being curbed. Law enforcement agencies and the government worked with YouTube to avoid malpractice. This was done to remove violent videos by terrorists promoting activities that could influence the viewers. Illegal and dangerous content was removed, and those that proved to be controversial were also removed.

## Evolution of YouTube as a Platform for Individuals and Companies

With the advent of YouTube in 2005, it became one of the greatest game changers of the Internet. It was beneficial to video producers, entertainment industrialists, and casting agents. They could now easily find sources of talent. If videos became a mega hit, then producers and agents contacted the video uploader to sign record deals and contracts. Since YouTube's inception, several "YouTube celebrities" have ended up becoming a worldwide phenomena due to their homegrown talent. Many Hollywood companies and record labels have also been on the constant lookout and have partnered with YouTube for this very purpose. Several comedians, bloggers, and singers have been given recognition by celebrities, one notable example being Justin Bieber through Usher. Several celebrities also created channels to increase their fame. Celebrities who were conventionally popular through traditional media also received invitations from the team at YouTube to upload videos, increasing the amount of traffic to the site and growing their target audience and followers to a far greater extent than what they obtained through their TV shows and movies.

In the year 2006, YouTube also partnered with NBC and promoted TV shows aired by NBC. Following this came the purchase of YouTube by Google, for $1.65 billion. This served as a good platform to market products, and advertising companies flocked the scene. Thus, marketing professionals of big companies fled from the television screen to the Internet. Soon YouTube became customer-driven and business-driven. Independent artists, singers, and comedians were able to milk the crowd with little-to-no cost. Four big record labels came into play though they were all very apprehensive given the large amount of copyrighted content that was on the site. YouTube provided a platform to these big record label companies by creating a partnership with them. The lucrative offer was that the site served as a base to make more money for these record labels. In 2009, YouTube partnered with Vivendi and formed Vevo. Vevo was a music service video channel.

YouTube also provided a platform for several channels to increase their profits by investing $875,000 in NextUp, which was a training and tips program for prospective users of YouTube. The company also used celebrities and icons to promote the channel, hoping to get the best of both worlds.

YouTube also was a free platform to test and promote music labels. Videos were categorized as mega, mainstream, and mid sized, which got rave reviews from target audiences. With this, recording artists could test songs before releasing them for free. This increased the amount of hits. YouTube also made its policies very strict as its popularity grew. In 2014, YouTube started to block videos from labels that flouted rules and were not a part of the paid subscription, and they lead to bad reviews and loss of profits.

## Video Uploading: Means of Livelihood

In 2007, YouTube launched its very first Partner Program. This was an advertisement revenue-sharing concept that had about 30,000 partners by 2012. Some of the top partners earned about $100,000 annually and others earned much more than just this. Brands that wanted to advertise were to pay the partners money of up to six figures to create and upload ads that would come on their channel.

## Relations between the Citizens and the Government:

YouTube has been constantly working to bridge the gap between the citizens of the US and the government. For instance, in the 2007 Presidential debates, people were encouraged to submit questions to the US presidential candidates via a YouTube video. Since visual images prove to be stronger, creating a better impact than mere words, the New York Times journalist Katharine Q. Seelye stated that videos have the power to impact people, and responses in the form of videos can create gusto, influence, and can even shape the way elections are being portrayed. Politics today have been shaped by the Internet, and with video browsing being an available option, candidates are able to channel their views to gain favor among the public. The US Presidential elections are connected with videos, and many presidential candidates have opted to engage the public through YouTube videos. This has enabled the youth to be more actively involved in politics. The youth have also been more participative, and the onset of videos has caused a spurt in the number of voters. The videos have profoundly affected the channel of the elections and have linked the population together with demographic barriers being broken down.

Today, television advertising is still prominent and is still considered an ideal way through which politicians can influence the masses. However, with better resources being channeled towards Internet advertising, more audiences have been reached. The elections saw that only 10 percent of the total budget for advertising was channeled towards the Internet, and it proved to be a grand success. YouTube helped to facilitate communication and engage the public, who were also able to share their thoughts and views and participate actively. Volunteering, funding, financing, and other campaigning formats could be reached due to YouTube. When the public decided to share and give good ratings to the videos, it was more influential as opposed to the advertising done by campaigners. This increased credibility and enhanced public image of the politicians.

Many government entities and important bodies used YouTube as a medium to give out information. Regular news feeds, updates, and important announcements were featured on the channels on the website. In fact, the officially verified YouTube channel of the White House was one of the largest producers of news and dissemination of information to the public. Barack Obama's presidency was a widespread topic to talk about and gained massive YouTube popularity. The impact created by users of YouTube was something that was quite admirable. In fact, politicians became more cautious about what they said, as did journalists and other public speakers. This was done to avoid being mocked or parodied by users.

Today, politicians and celebrities are more accessible than they were in the previous era. Communication from their side is a lot easier, but at the same time, undesirable questions could also be dodged. Videos were created to communicate to the electorate directly. The spontaneity of politics was now gone and replaced by more carefully planned and well-thought-out strategies.

Several government agencies have been actively exploring the ways through which they can use YouTube for their needs. In 2014, a meeting was held with several prominent YouTube celebrities, along with the US President Obama, to find ways through which it was possible to connect with youth. Now, presidents could easily connect with people through videos posted to their channels. The exposure afforded by prominent YouTube celebrities also helped to formulate opinion and gain votes. Social media platforms were also explored and given way to make the Affordable Healthcare Act (ACA or "Obamacare") more accessible. Youth were persuaded and recruited to enroll in ACA health insurance through YouTube videos and spoofs. The

President also organized interviews with famous YouTube celebrities to engage the public and to connect with the crowd. Other government entities include water supplying agencies, social welfare agencies, and government programs that list announcements, contests, awareness, and courses to empower the citizens.

## Engagement between individuals and private institutions

Educational institutions, private bodies, and firms have found ways to actively engage the audience. Companies create videos to attract the younger generation into joining them, creating a prospective platform to channel resources. These firms have modified their regulations to attract the "YouTube generation." Law firms have played an active role in this. They have created videos to help people to understand and follow the law, to join their firms, and to throw light on what life is like at the firms. The videos have also shown communication from employees and showed how client visits work. Universities have also managed to seek the younger generation through videos. They use this resource as a way to communicate with students and encourage people to apply to the university. These videos are more extensive for they shed light on the various strategies through which people can gain admissions, the criteria colleges look for in applicants, and the campus life, along with publishing question-and-answer sessions. Sample lectures, insights to courses, and information about the college are also common YouTube video topics for universities.

## Broadened Expression of Political Ideas

YouTube is an advocate of democracy. This was one of the reasons why it won the George Foster Peabody Award in 2008. It was a place where people could share their opinions, especially in the political domain. Studies done by the Pew Research Center showed that protest was amongst the second most viewed and spoken about topic among video uploaders. This only came second to news and information disseminated by agencies. Protesters have often uploaded videos showing the negative side of a story.

One of the most prominent instances of this is the Arab Spring. In one video, protestors showed injustice done by the political leaders. This created an impact as the ideologies of the protestors gained international recognition. People now use YouTube as a platform to voice their views and plant the seed of truth for the viewers across the world.

This led to the banning of YouTube by several countries. The government agencies of many countries wanted to reduce the exposure of such content to the public, as it tended to cause social unrest and political uprising. Many government bodies also became apprehensive of YouTube. Though this violated the ethics of the people, any video that mocked the national leaders and diplomats was to be taken down. Governments of countries like Syria investigated all the videos pertaining to Syria uploaded on YouTube, and uploaders of videos with faulty content were arrested. Thus, in 2012, to protect the identities of users, YouTube came up with a blur tool which could blur the faces of subjects to avoid identification or recognition.

Those countries that restricted users from certain acts like mockery, parody, and comedy found freedom in YouTube. They could now post videos that were acceptable without getting into trouble. People could also talk about their personal opinion on the government, its agendas, and its policies. Satires about news articles and political parties became a common phenomenon. One such video was the satiric video showing the "Arrest of Vladimir Putin: A Report From the Courtroom," which became a sensation. It was featured on the YouTube homepage for about two weeks.

Through YouTube, politicians and government agencies also are able to channel their viewers into constructive things. Kony 2012, a video featuring the International Criminal Court inductee Joseph Kony, was posted on YouTube causing widespread anger and led to protests favoring the demise of Joseph Kony. The video by Invisible Children, Inc. received about 84 million views in a span of 17 days. This served as an example of how YouTube revolutionized political debate and got the government involved. Subsequently resulting online movements rose up as well.

## Benefits of Sharing Personal Information

Several videos came about where users started to be more vocal about their sexual orientation. After the US military's "Don't ask, don't tell" policy, several videos that spoke about the user's opinions and support came about. This was mainly done to spread awareness, increase support, prevent suicide, and create like-mindedness. YouTube developed a way through which people could select their viewers. With this, users could limit how their videos could be watched by people. This mitigated stigma about sharing personal information. Several older generations have also made use of the video platform provided by YouTube to share their life stories. Met with positive views, many videos took a biographical or an autobiographical turn. This broke down barriers, and people were better able to connect with others.

## Dangers of Sharing Personal Information

However, there have been videos that have been flagged as inappropriate. These videos include those that contain discussions of a user's self-harm or suicidal tendencies. These tend to have a negative impact on users and can become a form of culture for youth. With YouTube's highly influential ability, such videos can trigger self-harm, suicide, violent behavior, and protests. Regularity of viewing can affect mindsets. Opinionated videos that advocate a certain form of culture can cause humiliation and physical harm. These motivate a one-sided view.

One such video was the beating up of a female cheerleader by teenagers of a school that resulted in the loss of her sight and hearing. Violent videos were always discouraged. These usually gain media attention, and such videos also inspired documentaries by NGOs that advocated the rights of people. There are many cases where popular users have abused their status by manipulating their fans. False accounts and videos have been created, which have altered the mindsets of the fans both emotionally and physically. Many of these go unreported though a few have gained attention. Videos have also triggered suicide, murders, and theft.

## Advertising and Marketing

YouTube also has played a pivotal role in advertisement and marketing. It has been able to generate views and hits for small companies who have come to play. Previously, only large companies with enough resources could advertise on the main screen. Today, smaller companies can create channels, track their videos, check their views, promote their products, and appear on the main screen as well. The videos can also feature instructional content on the products that the company is promoting. These videos reduce the amount of resources required to be spent training customers and generate maximum attention towards the product.

The team at YouTube is also constantly trying to revolutionize advertising. By creating similar channels, and grouping products and similar companies together, they are working extensively towards obtaining content and videos easily for the end user.

## Measurement of Mainstream Opinion

YouTube also serves as a way by which people's opinion can be measured. Videos usually have a view counter that tells the user how many hits their video has received. Apart from just this, the comments section in the video gives one an idea of how the public responds to the content. In fact, the more views a video gets, the more attention it has attracted. This was specific in the cases of popular cover songs, how-to videos, and so on, wherein celebrities, recording companies, and production houses advocated and promoted those videos. Though several companies acknowledged that one could not gauge the popularity of the videos or the attention span of the target audience, they nonetheless promoted music videos. Video hits weren't necessarily a mark of fanatic attachment, but there were more concrete forms to measure this through sale of CDs and records. However, view count has been a faithful meter to understand the dynamics of the population. Additionally, in order to obtain more sales in concert tickets and promotional merchandise, videos have played a significant role.

In 2013, the YouTube Music Awards were created, which were solely based on the amount of hits that a particular artist received. Thus, it was the public who decided the amounts of votes and the winner instead of judges. It has also known to grow audiences, increase the levels of talent amongst people, and generate bigger revenue for the entertainment industry.

*Andrew Mckinnon*

# Chapter 3
# Earning Money from YouTube

All right, so pretty much everyone using the Internet is familiar with what a rage YouTube is at the moment. And it is quite easy to understand why YouTube has gained so much popularity so fast. You can find videos telling you almost everything about almost everything on YouTube. There are all sorts of tutorials, funny videos, videogame walkthroughs, stories, songs, and much more. Not only that, YouTube is not like your TV or any other video sharing platform. You have the chance to watch what you like, when you like, and you don't have to wait for it to start. You can pause, stop, rewind, and do what you want with it. It is like your personal TV that you can watch anytime that you like.

There are many advantages that YouTube has to offer, some of which are discussed in detail below.

YouTube has some inherent advantages over other platforms:

1)   Google owns YouTube. This means that a video uploaded on YouTube will be given preference over a video uploaded on some other video hosting website while displaying search results on Google. This is probably the biggest advantage of all. It is a risk that your video will get lost in the sea of videos that are present on the Internet, but that problem is effectively mitigated on YouTube. There is no danger of your video getting lost anywhere, and, in fact, it might end up being the first search result on Google, which is a big plus.

2)   YouTube has the biggest market share in online streaming websites that allow users to upload their own content. Isn't it obvious that you have to choose the best to be the best? You have to choose YouTube if you wish to get noticed and make it big online.

3)   YouTube is well connected to other social media, like Google+. It was a smart move on both Google and

YouTube's part to merge. They both benefitted from it but more so Google, as they now own one of the biggest Internet entities and amassed a lot of visitors.

4)    YouTube is extremely creator friendly, providing creators with lots of useful tools to analyze views on their channels and their videos. The user interface is extremely friendly, and everything is clear. There is no confusion and it is easy to choose a function. You have the chance to share, embed, stop, replay, pause, and jump to another video with the click of a button.

Now that we have read up on the various advantages of using YouTube as a platform to upload your video through your channel, let us look at what channels are all about.

In this chapter, I'll go over some tips and techniques to help you easily create a YouTube channel, create valuable content, build an audience, and earn revenue from your videos.

## Research

The first thing you need to do before starting a YouTube channel is research. You have to take a look at the different types of content available on YouTube and look for topics that interest you and seem doable. See what works in reaching people and what doesn't. You also have to do your research on the competition. Check out all the channels available that are already doing what you intend to do. See what kind of subscribers they have, what sort of videos they post, and how (if at all) they interact with the subscribers. You have to decide on at least two or more topics, so that you have the chance to pick the best one for your channel. Don't choose something that already has a lot of videos and subscribers. You need something that is still a relatively new topic and one where there are not many videos on it. Don't choose something that is drab and dull, and go for topics that are intriguing. The basic idea is to show people something that they have yet to come across before or show them something better than what they already have seen.

## Basics of Copyrights

YouTube is a huge platform where millions of people share videos. Obviously, sometimes similar-looking content can run into copyright-related problems. You need to know that you are protected by copyright if you upload original content, and if you upload someone else's original content, they are protected by copyright. YouTube has a very strict and vigilant copyright enforcement process, and if you come across a video that has stolen your content, you can send a complaint to YouTube, and they will take care of the issue.

Sometimes, you can buy content legally from someone else. YouTube has a Content ID tool which searches and blocks videos that contain material from someone else's video(s). If you have legal rights to content that you didn't actually create but bought from someone else, you can challenge this, and YouTube will look into the issue.

Another important concept to wrap your head around is the "Fair Use" clause. This clause allows people on YouTube to comment on, criticize, or remix your video in whatever way they want. You cannot take down such a video by sending them a copyright infringement notice. They'll just send you a counter notification. You can get into trouble for misusing the copyright infringement notification feature. I'm sure you have seen a sea of spoofs and also a river of bad comments. All this is part of YouTube, and you have to embrace it if you wish to use YouTube to your advantage.

## Metadata

Metadata is the information associated with the video that isn't included in the video itself. This includes the title, description, thumbnail, and tags. Metadata is important to provide for context, so YouTube can better help people find what they are looking for. So, say for example, you wish to make your video on cheesecakes become popular. You choose tags and a description that contains words which people are most likely to type into Google while looking for cheesecakes, such as cheese, cakes, blueberries, etc. Your metadata should be carefully considered if you want your video to turn up as the first search result on Google.

With that said, you should be aware that some people misuse this metadata to trick viewers or attract more attention to their videos. This is done by posting misleading or generic titles, false descriptions, inappropriate or misleading thumbnails, and by using unnecessary tags for categories that aren't relevant to the video. You must stay away from this practice as it is against the community guidelines. How many times have you clicked on something just because it has an interesting title and realized that the uploader has tricked you to simply click on the link and increase their viewership? This is intentional to try and have a large number of hits and start making money from it. But this is completely illegal. You cannot cheat people to make it big. This can result in takedown of your video and even termination of your account. Make sure you add only useful and relevant metadata, and don't try to play the search algorithm. You will only end up feeling disappointed and might lose out on the chance of making it big on the Internet by indulging in unfair practices.

## Types of Content That Can Be Monetized

The best way to ensure you can monetize your YouTube videos is to create all of your visual and audio content by yourself. Being original is very helpful. Create the soundtracks, logos, footage, animation, and/or any other stuff by yourself, and make sure you still own the rights to all of it. This makes sure you can earn money from your video.

If you created all the content of the video yourself but don't own the rights to it, you cannot monetize the video. For example, a musician can't monetize a video with their own music in the soundtrack if they are in a record deal where the record label owns all the commercial rights to their music.

If you use any content you created with the help of software, you can monetize it only if the license of your software allows for commercial usage of the material created. You may need to submit additional information to YouTube, too. If you use loops, music samples, or stock images, you have to mention this expressly and know if you are allowed to use them commercially. Even if you have your video up for a few days, you will not be able to escape the eyes of people who own the software. You surely don't want to get into trouble and so must choose the right path.

Creative Commons or royalty-free content can also be monetized given that the actual creator of the content has allowed for it. Sometimes, you need written permission to use it. But if you have picked it from public domain, then there might be no such restrictions.

Tutorials explaining how to use a particular software or walkthroughs of games are highly dependent on the software or game itself to see if they can be monetized. If you are allowed to show the interface to the public for commercial use, you can monetize the video. Don't simply jump into something just to start off with it. Understand the necessities and see if you have the rights to monetize the video before you start with it.

Recordings from TV, DVD, public concerts, and events can only be monetized if the actual artist or creator of the content gives you written permission to do so. This is because while the recording may be yours, the content is still mostly the other person's property, and they own the rights to it. There are many that try and get as many people as possible to watch something before they get caught. However, if they are barred from uploading again, then what is the point of amassing several views and subscribers? So, think it through before you do something.

Content found online also cannot be monetized usually, even if it is free. The commercial rights usually rest with the actual creator of the material.

So, these are the various rules to adhere to when you wish to monetize videos and if there is content belonging to others. You really must not take anything for granted as there is a lot of awareness now, and other content owners are constantly waiting for an opportunity to take someone down, and you sure don't want to get into such trouble.

## Finding Your Niche

YouTube is no small community. There is an abundance of creators as well as viewers, all of them with variegated interests, passions, and needs. This comes into play while you decide to make your videos or upload content through your channel. It is normal to feel that making videos about the most trending and wide-reaching topics will make your videos better and will reach a larger number of people, but many a times, it has been seen that videos that cater to a niche audience perform better than generic ones. In fact, many YouTube channels have achieved success by making videos for a niche audience. They will see whatever is trending and decide to put out videos that fall into the particular category. Similarly, look for videos that you think are doing well. However, you will have to make it extremely good as there is already a lot of competition for it.

The great thing about finding your niche and making videos about it is that you are actually interested in the topic, and this makes it that much easier for you to create the video. You are more driven and passionate about it. You can connect better with the fans. All of this leads to a higher success rate. So, instead of following the herd, try and make videos about something that *you* love and care about. You may think that a particular topic is too obscure to be liked by too many people, but sometimes it's surprising how many people are interested in such topics. There is no point in giving people something that they have already seen. Try offbeat topics and things that will easily grab people's attention. You cannot play it safe if you wish to make it big. Choose topics that you think will draw in crowds that like to view different things.

## Favoring Series Over Oneshots

See, one-off videos are great, and they can help you get a lot of views in a short amount of time if they go viral, but they are not really sustainable. Your views graph on YouTube will spike suddenly and then fall rapidly if you only have one popular one-off video. It is like being a one-hit wonder. You will have one popular song or video that people will love, and then you will disappear because nothing else will click with the audience.

On the other hand, series or shows can be quite powerful in helping you gain and keep your subscribers. If you create a recurrent theme and keep your viewers excited every time, you can have a loyal fan base that constantly grows and eagerly waits for your videos. You will see that it is possible for people to jump from one video to another, and all your videos will be displayed on the right-hand side of the page. So, you will have the chance to present a lot of videos to the same viewer. This will increase your reach and get more and more people to see what you have and get them to subscribe.

## Shareability

The most important question you need to ask yourself before you make a video is,

"Will people share this?"

Now of course, you may tell yourself,

"Why wouldn't they? My video is going to be awesome!"

That's A++ enthusiasm right there, and it's great - but it's not always practical. It has very little to do with what *you* think of it but what *others* will. You need to think about how people will react to your video and what will happen once you put your video out there. You need to have some insights on what kind of stuff people like to share and what they do not. For instance, take a look at the last few posts you or your friends have shared on any of your social networks. This will give you a fair idea on what the trends are regarding sharing. People need to relate to your videos on some level to want to share them. One key thing to keep in mind while doing this is whether your video adds value to the viewer's life in any way (humor, knowledge, how-to). If so, then it is more likely to be shared by the viewer. Here it is tough to assess as what is humorous for you might not be for others and what is educational and inspirational to you may not be for others. So, the plan is to try and find out what will really interest them. For this, you have to look at samples that are already available on the site. Say, for example, there are 20 videos on a topic. There will be just one or two that will be on top and have the most views. You have to see what sets them apart from the rest. Is it the language used, the style of presentation, or something else? You must also decide on shooting your video in a similar fashion, but don't copy. Nobody fancies something that is copied. You have to be as original as possible if you wish to make it big in the world of YouTube.

Another thing you may want to think about is the summary of your video. If the concept of your video is easily explainable in a few words or a couple of sentences, the chances of it being shared increase. Complex ideas turn people off as they shy away from explaining it all to other people. However, if you take a tough concept and explain it easily, then people will fall for it. They will think of it as an opportunity to explain it well enough to others. So, it is up to you to choose the right type of video to upload and get more and more people to watch it.

## Direct Conversation

If you want to get your viewers more involved in your videos, you need to talk to them. Conversation is a great way to bond with the viewers and make them feel like a part of your videos and your channel. Many YouTube channels use this and address the users directly in their videos.

I am sure you have seen a lot of people all having conversations. Here, the uploader will also actively participate in the conversations. This is a great way to understand what people want. Say, for example, you have put up a video on impersonations. You want to know if you are doing a good job at it. For this, you have to solicit the response of the audience. You will have to ask them questions and seek answers for it. There will be a lot of idiots out there who will only comment because they have no other work to do. But you should simply ignore them and talk to the ones who are genuinely interested in giving you a feedback. Don't sit around and reply to everybody who is talking to you; speak only with those that are genuinely interested in giving feedback.

You can also just specifically address a certain kind of audience that watches your videos or that is special to you. Sometimes, you can even call a particular viewer out by their name, ask for suggestions, and do some shout-outs, among other things. This is important to connect with the viewers. You don't need to do this in every video. Some users do short Q&A sessions every once in a while, others use fictional characters from their series to talk to the fans. Be creative and come up with your own ways to talk to the viewers as they are the stars of the show, and you will make it big in this business only if you have their support. Try and find as many people as possible to support you. If you think someone is purposely hounding you, then choose to ignore them and don't fuel their enthusiasm by responding to them. They are there only to steal your audience, and chances are they own a channel that puts out similar videos as you and are only trying to discourage you.

## Discoverability

Discoverability refers to your video's potential to be found through search results or related videos. You must've noticed that some videos show up on the sidebar when you are watching a video, after you're done watching it. These are known as related videos and are a powerful way to get better reach. Say, for example, you just finished watching an artist's music video on the side bar. You will see other popular videos of the same artist, as well as those of others. Once your video ends, there will be more suggestions that will show up on the screen. This is important because you need to see everything that is being offered for you to watch and not stop at just one. Imagine having to type the same type of search again - would that not be boring and tedious? To remedy this issue, YouTube provides these links.

To increase your video's discoverability, optimize your title and description in the best possible way without breaking community policies and pay attention to the types of topics. There are topics that are temporary, like holidays and elections, and then evergreen ones, like tutorials and pop culture icons. You need to make efficient use of these topics in your videos to gain more viewers. You know how it is possible to appear on top of the search list and why getting there is extremely important. Be aware and use the SEO metadata wisely to show up on top.

## Interactivity

The best way to make your audience enjoy the video is to make them feel like they are actually a *part* of it! Interactivity is all about making your videos two dimensional instead of just one. If people feel like it's one sided, they won't connect as well with the video, and even if they do, they won't be too compelled to wait for another video.

YouTube, fortunately, is a very interactive platform. You can answer fan questions, take suggestions from them, feature their videos or channels in yours, and even ask them questions. These are some great ways to involve them and make them feel like a part of your channel. Pay attention to the audience's likes and dislikes. Interacting with your audience gives them the feeling that you care about their opinions. You must ask them to tell you what they want so that you can create it for them. Once you start to please the audience, they will start liking your channel more and more. All you have to do is please your audience in order to get them to subscribe to you. Don't simply provoke your subscribers to all fight with each other. That might cost you your viewers. Make it as fun and interactive as possible and get more and more people to watch your videos and subscribe to you.

## Consistency

Consistency is of the essence when it comes to gaining and maintaining your subscribers and views on YouTube. This doesn't necessarily mean consistency of schedule, which creates anticipation among your viewers, but can also mean consistency of themes, personality, format, or other things. These aspects keep people interested. If you suddenly put up unrelated videos, then it will only confuse your subscribers. You must not change your channel up but need to maintain consistency so that people remember what your channel is all about. If you wish to diversify your channel, then wait for some time, and don't do all of it at once. Add in videos on new topics only if your subscribers have said ok to it. You have to please them in order to hold on to them. So, remain consistent in your theme and, more importantly, with the quality of your videos.

## Collaboration

Collaborating with other YouTube creators is a great way to boost your fan base. It not only makes the video *that* much more awesome for the subscribers of both the channels, but it also helps you brainstorm ideas in a better way and create higher quality stuff. It's a win-win scenario where your subscribers are introduced to the other person's audience, and their subscribers are introduced to yours. But remember, there should be equality. You cannot collaborate with someone that has only a few viewers. You would end up getting only a few from theirs, and all yours will subscribe to theirs, which is not fair. You need someone who has at least as much as you or slightly more. But if you think their work is under-appreciated and there is a lot of potential to increase your viewer base by a large margin, then you can go ahead and collaborate with them. But remember, you have to work everything out before you collaborate in order to avoid any discrepancies. You have to get everything well sorted and ready before you put out the videos together.

Finally, you must keep in mind that the above-mentioned points are not a sort of checklist that you need to strike off to be successful. They are all useful in some way or another but don't necessarily need to be used together for creating a great channel. Be innovative and figure out what works for you. Don't follow the herd; try and do what you think is right. Once you earn a few favorable views, your confidence will get boosted, and you will have the chance to add in more videos and garner a bigger crowd for yourself.

*Andrew Mckinnon*

# Chapter 4
# Benefits of Using YouTube for Business

Before you go about setting up your own channel, take a look at how exactly it will help you. Once you get a good grasp of all the benefits of using this platform, you will definitely be signing up without any more coaxing required.

YouTube has grown magnificently since its launch and has a huge audience all over the world, wherever Internet is available. This makes it one of the best forms of media to generate audiences for just about any purpose.

It is quite evident that over the years, people have shown a tendency to prefer visual content over reading material. Thus, video content has garnered a huge following and easily engages people.

## Easy Interface

The website is extremely easy to use and thus has easy accessibility. Content is generated on the homepage according to the user's preferences and in a huge range of languages. Any layman who doesn't have much knowledge on computers and the Internet can easily use YouTube. It is not rocket science; it's extremely convenient for people to find what they are looking for. It is also extremely easy for people to search for something they want, to share the video, rate it, like it, dislike it, write comments, respond, and more. The ease of use makes this website the most preferred to watch videos on the Internet.

## Large Audience

If the video is really engaging, the audience it generates is also larger. The more a person likes the video, the better the chance that they will share it with others. This acts as a way to keep increasing the audience for the video. And due to the increasing accessibility of Internet over the world, the potential for generating audience is growing even more. The accessibility of videos on YouTube is even greater because the content can easily be played on a variety of devices like mobile phones or tablets. So, the accessibility is extremely large. Will you not want your video to be seen by millions of people or will you be happy with a few thousand? If you have a million watching, then you will have the chance to increase your profit several fold. So, choosing YouTube is your best bet if you wish to make it big with online video sharing. The search engine of YouTube falls behind only Facebook and Google and has billions of daily views.

## Preference for Video Format

As we already mentioned, most people prefer watching video content rather than reading about something. Thus, you can attract more people with a good video rather than by making them read a bunch of text, which has no allure whatsoever. This is why most websites try to host video content in order to get a larger number of visitors. Everything can be converted into a video, and there are simply no restrictions on it. Right from text to speech to videos to audio, everything can be translated into the video format and uploaded. You will have the chance to reach audiences with special needs as well, and it will become extremely convenient for you to increase your subscriber base if you cater to the majority of audience by giving them content they would like to find.

## Demonstration

The video can be used to demonstrate the exact use of the product or service you are advertising. This helps the customer to see the product in action and be more convinced about purchasing it. If it is a person, they can even demonstrate their skills and show the customer what they have to offer. This is especially useful for electronics and cosmetics. Imagine having to buy a juicer without knowing how it performs. There is no way for you to test something if you are buying it online. In fact, you can't test a juicer at the store either. So, this can be remedied by watching a video that is uploaded by the maker to demonstrate how the juicer works. Similarly, there are a lot of other products out there that are not easily understood by people. Take, for example, cosmetics. People might not know to use a particular type of mascara or a curler. If there is a video demonstration for these, then it will be extremely easy for people to understand, and chances of them buying the product will greatly increase.

## Visual Impact

Video content can be used to reach out to people on a deeper level than nearly any other tool. A video with the right content, which reaches out to the audience, leaves a more lasting impression. This is why companies have been making more and more advertisements, which play with the right mix of emotions to attract the audience. It is easier to convey a message through a video than by making people read about it. There is also the possibility of influencing them in a better way.

Say, for example, you wish to advertise an ice cream. If you simply distribute pamphlets listing out its wonderful taste, then nobody will buy it. However, if you make a video featuring a woman enjoying the ice cream and you show the product and all its layers, then you will be sold out in no time. So, it is important to make use of videos to promote something as opposed to writing it down for someone to read. So, accordingly, videos on YouTube can be used more effectively for conveying a message. The more you add a personal touch, the more people will tend to buy into it. This will automatically generate a larger following based on the trust factor.

## Inexpensive

Making a video can be quite inexpensive, and thus your investment is minimal. You can even make a simple yet effective video with the help of your smart phone as long as it has a camera. Since more and more devices have been developing good camera features, it has become fairly easy to make your own video. Another great feature that makes this easier is all the different photography applications, which help to enhance the quality and content of such videos to attract a larger audience. All you have to do is shoot it and enhance it to get more and more people to like it. Even if your initial investment is "0," you have the chance to make a lot of money through your videos. Imagine how much money can come your way if you make it big by uploading videos that people want to see? So, don't waste any more time thinking about what to upload and get uploading at the earliest!

## Re-Purposed Content

The content you create can be re-purposed into different formats. You can use them as podcasts, video series, and more to reach different audiences based on what they prefer. Thus, you can engage more people with a small effort. Again, all of this is free for you. All that you are doing is creating videos in an inexpensive manner and spreading them around. You will ultimately have a lot of places where your video will be present to get more and more people to view it. That is exactly how several Americans have turned into millionaires. They have made use of technology to help them in capitalizing on what they have to offer to the world. You, too, can become extremely successful if you put your mind to it and try and make a quick buck out of your passion for the Internet.

## Email Listing

The software on Google allows an easy way to get more email listings. You can embed a sign-up form for your listing directly into a video. When a person is viewing the video, they can enter their own email ID and subscribe. This helps in increasing your email list massively. So, you can send out reminders, add in links to new videos, and keep your audience updated. Gone are the days when you had to find out someone's email address. All you have to do now is get them to give it away themselves. Isn't that extremely convenient? You don't have to run behind an audience, and instead, they will run behind you. Even if some of them unsubscribe from your mails, you will always have your loyal subscribers who will be ever present to view something that you suggest.

## AdWords and AdSense

The program AdSense is used for generating money from advertisements on the content of the website. This is done on the basis of clicks or impression. By using AdSense, the user uploading the advertisements gets 55% of the generated revenue while the rest is earned by Google itself. The advertisements are served using technology, which studies the location, Internet history of the user, and so on. This is discussed in detail in a further chapter.

As you can see, there are many advantages to using YouTube for the purpose of business. You can earn from it with minimal investment or effort from yourself.

# Chapter 5
# Maximizing Profits

Any business needs customers for it to be successful no matter what their products or services are. The main reason for using YouTube for business or earning money is that it provides such huge potential for customers by means of its enormous audience. We already learned how to monetize from YouTube. Let us now look at how we can get more from YouTube.

## Advertisements

YouTube has a partner program, which allows publishers to run advertisements on videos. In exchange for this, YouTube gets a percentage of the revenue generated from these ads. The YouTube Partner Program can be used to generate income through this method. Some users believe that the publisher should revert to the program and start publishing ads a little while after starting their channel. First, gain an audience and subscribers based on the quality of content. This will keep them on for the long haul. You can then put in ads without your viewers getting annoyed. They have higher chances of staying online and watching the complete video including the ad. The Partner Program is usually available to those who have generated a specifically large number of views on their videos in a given amount of time.

It is irrelevant to you whether the subscriber has bought anything from the advertiser or has watched the video fully or not. All you care about is putting in the ad first, and your money is generated. You can tie up with as many companies as you like, and it will depend on how many videos you have to offer the public.

Signing up for these is fairly easy. You just need to give some PayPal or bank account details for the transactions to take place.

## Creative Videos

Making a good video is essential no matter how you intend to earn the money. If you are using the YouTube channel to promote your business, then make a catchy video about it. Utilize the skills and creativity of your team to make a video, which has the potential to go viral. Integrate your product or service into a storyline that will help the viewer connect with both together. Just having a good story won't help in marketing your product. On the other hand, having a boring video, which simply displays your product, won't catch any attention at all. This is why you need to show the viewer a creative display, which helps them connect with what you are offering. There are many things that you can do to make your video interesting. This includes adding in animation, sound effects, and, if you have good connections, then there's nothing like getting a celebrity involved. Your video might end up becoming viral, and this will only promote your business and products. Have a look at what is currently popular and selling like hot cakes in the market. You can incorporate the same concept in your videos and make them just as popular, if not more so. But remember, you have to aim high if you wish to make it big in this business. If your goals are large enough, then you will have the chance at making it really big. But if they are mediocre, then it is useless. Aim to reach the moon, and you will surely get to the stars.

## Search Engine Optimization

SEO refers to the visibility of a website or video or any result in particular in a search engine. Simply put, SEO is what decides if your video should be displayed in the first few results when the user searches for something. It works with the help of a really complex algorithm that Google came up with. All of that does not matter to you. What matters is what *you* can do to make sure your video appears in the list when the search engine is used, preferably within the top 5 results, as most people do not search beyond the first ten or fifteen videos. With regards to a Google search, almost no one uses page 2 to search for what they want. This alone should emphasize the importance of bringing your video up to the top few.

There are a few keywords that you can use to make sure a Google search displays the videos related to those keywords first in the results page after the search button is hit. These are known as "Video Keywords." This is important because not all of the traffic you get in a video is from a YouTube search. Google searches can help boost your viewership, but you need to be accurate with your video keywords. You need to research and find out what these words are. An example is "dance moves." It only makes sense that a video result would be preferred to a written article when it comes to dancing. Another example would be "dog tricks." It goes without saying that you need to find words that are related to your niche. Use these words in your tags, and make sure to also include them in your description, which should be as long as possible without boring the audience.

Getting a good number of "likes" on your video also makes YouTube's algorithm give preference to your video over others. Always leverage your "Call to Action" options, and ask your viewers to like, share, and subscribe so you have a better chance of getting your videos displayed as the first result. This helps direct traffic towards your videos, which should your primary goal if you want to make your YouTube endeavors bring about a passive revenue to supplement your primary income.

## Tutorials and How-To Videos

Another popular search on YouTube is by users wanting to know how to use or do something. You can use this to your benefit and monetize the opportunity.

For instance, let's assume you have a business, which sells some tools. Make videos to show exactly how these tools can be used and why they are better than others. Engage the viewers with a clear yet entertaining video, which convinces them to go and buy your product.

Another way is to make such tutorials and sign up for the ads program on YouTube. The better your content, the more popular it gets. This will generate more money for you using the AdSense program.

Here are some ideas for it.

### *Recipes*

This is probably the most important theme on YouTube. Cooking a passion for many people, and there is a combination of both amateurs and professionals out there who are constantly looking to expand their culinary knowledge. If you are a good cook, then it is ideal for you to start taping your cooking and putting it on YouTube. You will have a lot of subscribers in no time. But you have to make dishes that are unique and complex but explained in an easy manner.

For example, you can make both an omelet and a meringue with eggs, but if you make a video for just the former, then you might not get too many views, but if you make a video for the latter, then there will be a lot of views for it. So, it is up to you to choose the theme and put videos that will generate a lot of views for you. You can introduce your subscribers to a new recipe on a weekly basis and keep their interest alive. There are also those who explain cocktails and mocktails, which allow people to prepare for parties. So, the options are unlimited, and all it takes is a little patience and thinking to come up with a super menu to introduce people to. Remember, only unique dishes will cut it and not standard ones.

### DIYs

The whole world now tries to go the DIY way. This stands for "Do it Yourself." Gone are the days when people had to rely on store-bought products. People now make soaps, detergents, clothes, decorative pieces, etc., all in the confines of their own home. There are many people who also go commercial with it, owing to attaining success in the field. Imagine the number of subscribers you can have if you put DIY videos of things that people really want to buy! This can be showpieces, clothes, detergents, cleaners, and so on; the sky is the limit when it comes to DIY. You also have the chance to show people how to do something, and, in parallel, tell them you have samples that they can buy or tools that you sell, so there is just no limit on the amount of money you can earn by making DIY videos and posting them on YouTube.

### Building Stuff

There are many men out there who would like to look at videos that will help them build something; say, for example, a guitar. It is not easy to build a guitar, and you need to look at a demonstration to learn it. This is possible if you look at a video on YouTube that explains how something is built. You can see what people are looking at and work on those products. From musical instruments to houses to floors to even cars, there is a tutorial for each and every thing and also many more such things that need to be originally demonstrated. So, you must decide to get your tools out and tape your building endeavors to teach people and make a quick buck out of it.

### Demonstrations

As was said earlier, it is important to show people something as opposed to telling them about it. You have to show people how something works if you want them to buy it. This can be anything from electronics to cosmetics to anything else that needs to be demonstrated. You will get a fair idea by looking at topics that are trending. You can choose to pick a product and demonstrate it to the best of your abilities. You don't have to be too technical about it, but if you are, then that's well and good. You can also explain math problems if you are good at it or teach another subject. Anything goes as long as it is legit and you are able to make a good video.

### Unboxing

There is a massive audience out there that wants to see people unbox things. This is because they will have the chance to look at the product and know if it is worth buying. Most people unbox electronics, collectibles, and other such big investments, and you can unbox anything that you think will interest people. Electronics already have a lot of competition out there, and there are many popular bloggers who get their hands on a device the earliest and demonstrate it. So, if you wish to do the same, then it is best that you choose a different language like your local language to explain the features of the device. Similarly, it's great if you are unboxing, say, collector Barbie dolls, and then explaining them in a local language, as there are already hundreds who are doing it in English.

### Cartoons

There is nothing like a few funny cartoons to grab people's attention. Who doesn't love cartoons? You must decide on an audience and make cartoons that will interest them. But remember that they need to be completely original, and you cannot copy anything. If you are good at drawing and story telling, then you can come up with interesting characters and post videos of your cartoons. You can pander to a wide audience that is a mix of both youngsters and older people. In fact, college kids will love cartoons, and you can try out anime. You can choose whatever works for you and make the best of your YouTube channel's potential.

### Music Videos

Music is all the rage these days. If you are a composer, then get playing and upload the video. There are many genres to pick from, and you can choose the one that is comfortable for you. Apart from coming up with your own music, you can also indulge in covers. People love covers and will appreciate it if it is like the original but has a few variations. You can look up trending songs and cover them in the best way possible. Upload it, and voila, you can draw in a lot of people. Again, don't copy anything. If it is a cover, then mention it clearly, and don't go around posting it as an original composition.

### Impersonations

Impersonations are extremely popular these days. From celebrities to sportsmen and actors, there are a lot of people who can be impersonated. There are some amazing ones out there that are making a lot of money through their videos. If you are good at emulating someone, then you can tape yourself and upload the videos. Characters from TV shows are quite popular, and you can choose a few that you think people will like. Remember, you must not think of anything as being silly as everything is interesting.

## Spoofs

There are a lot of spoofs of movie scenes, music videos, etc. You will have a lot of subscribers if you make people laugh by posting videos of spoofs and mock videos. You have to be on the lookout for songs that are really big right now and create spoof videos for them. But remember that you cannot copy any of the original content. You have to compose your music and make your own music video.

## Gags & Funny Videos

Videos that showcase gags or videos where someone has failed miserably while doing something are all extremely popular on YouTube. There is a whole world available for funny pet videos and the same goes for babies. People will give anything to get entertained by these, and all you have to do is shoot a funny video about your pet, child, or any other family member or friend and upload it.

Remember that you have to keep these separate and do not mix them all up. If you wish to mix them, then first gather a large enough audience for one type of videos and then move to others. If you try and do many things at once, then it might not work well for you. I'm sure you've heard of the phrase jack-of-all-trades master of none; you surely don't want that happening to you.

## *Workouts*

There is always a demand for home-based workouts as the 21st century sees more people doing most of their work from a computer or a phone. If you are a "fitness maniac," then this might be the best choice for you as you are earning money by helping people without charging them a dime, a complete win-win situation. Uploading circuits of workouts that you had performed while you were a beginner would definitely gain a huge number of viewers. Video logging is also another great way to gain more support as there is nothing better than real-life proof of the workouts actually having an effect. Be as supportive as you can be by replying to questions asked in comments and giving personal feedback to those who need it, and you are sure to become quite popular among those aspiring to be fit.

### *Gaming Guides*

Games are one of the few major applications of the Internet. There is no better platform than YouTube to get some tips and tricks in games if you are facing difficulties. Around 15% of YouTube's videos are related to games, which is clear proof that this topic is a goldmine for views. If you are a professional gamer, or even a person who plays games for the fun of it, then uploading walkthroughs, guides, and how-to's of specific mainstream games can help turn in lots of views. There is always a demand for cracking particular sections of a game efficiently. Newer games tend to be fast-paced with a huge gameplay time. Giving ideas on getting through the game easily will definitely aid with establishing a fan base. This essentially means you are increasing your profits with the help of Google AdSense.

### *Education Related*

With e-learning taking preference over traditional classroom teachings, your chance to profit from teaching will increase through YouTube videos. Most e-learning websites require students to pay for downloading or streaming their content. If you are a teacher proficient in a specific field, uploading videos related to that field will definitely gain attention, raking in more views. As it is mostly the younger generation students who opt for e-learning, your viewers should increase tremendously as no one uses social media platforms to share good quality educational material better than young students.

## *Trending Topics*

It is very easy to create fresh content related to trending topics. You can find some trending topics without difficulties via Facebook and Twitter. They always display such topics in the sides, and you can create content for videos based on some research. Another great place to get details on recent trends is Google itself. Facebook and Twitter show you recent trends, but you do not get to choose your field of interest. Google offers you the choice of selecting your own topics, so you can find trends related to your niche, be it science or sports or even Hollywood. Be careful, as these topics are usually debated by hot-blooded people, and you do not want to get on anybody's wrong side. Make sure to double-check the facts you state and mention at the end of the video that you did not mean any disrespect to anyone. Keep it diplomatic, offer solutions, make it catchy, and you can easily gain a large number of views with a wide audience who respect your opinions.

## Display Yourself as a Leader

Use the videos to show the viewers that you are a leader in your field. This can be done by showing skills in any area of expertise that your company deals with. Demonstrate these skills through videos. You can also put up videos, which are in the form of seminars to give advice or tips on just about anything.

# Chapter 6
# Marketing

The online presence of YouTube is huge, and it can be used for marketing just about anything if you know how to do it right. The basic point of viewers going to this website is to view videos, and keeping that in mind, you can use YouTube for marketing just about anything through videos.

If your budget can cover it, get experts for making a good marketing video for your company. Nothing can beat experience and their advice as well as expertise will help you get on the fast track to success. Once you make a high quality video, which the viewers will like, you're set. Look for someone who has already done good work for someone else. You can also ask someone who is creative to help you out if you are not able to afford the services of a professional. There is a lot of power in the wisdom shared by someone who is creative, and you need to take it seriously and employ someone who is well worth your time and effort to come up with a good video for you.

You then need to find the right keywords for drawing the viewers to your video. Use analysis for finding such keywords and target the right group of people from whom you can benefit. So, find the words that are best for your channel and use it to end up as the first search result in Google.

The success of your video will be marked by the number of views it gets in a given period of time. Like a spoof video going viral within a few minutes owing to it being extremely funny. You can even get help on this front to make sure that the video reaches the maximum number of people as soon as it is out. So, creativity is the key. You have to be as creative as possible and make use of funny taglines or something that will grab people's attention immediately and force them to share it with others.

You can also make a TrueView ad, which runs in the beginning of videos. Making a good advertisement, which has at least the first five seconds attract the viewer, will work to your benefit.

Keep a connection with the viewers. They will be leaving comments about the video or product in the comments section. Try to interact with them as much as possible and also show that their views matter. It will be interesting to see what people have to say about you and your videos, and you will have the chance to improve on your videos. This will keep them engaged with you on a personal front.

You can also create merchandise to sell on your products as well as the channel. Many companies have been selling things like mugs and t-shirts to advertise their products and share their channel. You have to pick up something from it that is catchy and popular. You have to get the words printed on your merchandise.

As we talk about marketing, another thing to keep in mind is that you need to market the videos you put on your channel as well. Try to generate as much traffic for your channel as you possibly can. For this, you need to have a good online presence. So, you can paste the videos on your

Facebook page or your Twitter and get more and more people to like it.

Many websites allow you to embed the YouTube URL for your video onto their platform. This allows you to display your content on other sites as well. The user doesn't necessarily have to go on YouTube to view it. Just put the link to your video on any forum, which is relevant to your content, and promote it. You can also connect links from different places so that the viewer gets directed to your YouTube channel if they click it. Research and find as many forums which are related to your content and will let you promote on their page. Take part in the discussions there and get links to your videos posted on these.

Sharing links on other channels in YouTube will also help you in getting more views. If the channels have similar content, then your viewers will be more focused on their interests in the same type of content as well.

You should also share the video without any privacy settings in order to get the maximum views that can possibly be generated for it. Closing any section will limit your view count as well.

Find ways to get as many people directed to your YouTube channel as possible. Get other websites or blogs to use your channel link on their homepage so that your video gets more views. On a small-scale effort, you can even make cyber hubs make your URL their homepage. This way, anyone who logs in will first see your video.

You can also use VidCon for help in this front. It is a huge group of people who create online videos and others who are somehow linked to this. Utilize their opinions and expertise in optimizing your channel on YouTube. This forum helps you connect to a large group of people who can help you on many fronts while promoting your video as well.

Use different social media platforms like Facebook to create a community for your YouTube channel. This way, you can share your videos on such platforms and allow viewers to interact there as well. It just opens another place for you to monetize on your video.

Remember that you can help your business grow really big if you put your mind to it. You have to know exactly how to use YouTube to your advantage. Don't simply copy someone else, and try and be as unique as possible. Once you get the hang of it, you will start adding in more and more videos that will benefit you and your company. If you cannot afford the services of a professional to shoot a video for you, then enlist the services of the most creative people in your company. They will help you in not just creating the best videos but also help you save a buck. The possibilities are endless when it comes to using YouTube to promote something, and you have to do your best to find the right way for things to be done.

While talking about social media, it will be worthwhile to mention YouTube. It is a popular website for uploading personal videos free of cost. YouTube is one of the topmost sites having the maximum number of hits in the world. In the IPL-3 T20 cricket tournament in India, YouTube collaborated with IPL for the live streaming of the cricket matches. Although not expected, this idea turned out to be an instant hit during the tournament. Although it was meant mainly for the viewers outside India, it was surprising to note that the site had maximum number of hits from India. The site got more than 49.5 million hits (Kincaid, 2010), which was way beyond YouTube's expectation. This was a golden opportunity for companies to promote themselves. Soon, lots of companies (premium brands like Idea, HP, USL, HSBC and Coca Cola) flocked around to provide sponsorship for the whole IPL season and to promote their brands via online advertising during the IPL matches. Companies grabbing such opportunities will be the ones having a competitive advantage in the digital world.

The concept of STP (Segmentation Targeting Positioning) is an old one in marketing and is one of the most important to be followed. If the targeting part is seen, then YouTube provides a very useful tool. It has a link called the YouTube Video Targeting Tool. With this tool, any company is allowed to broadcast its ads in a particular country or it can choose to broadcast it worldwide. So, a company can very easily apply the concepts of Product Specialization by advertising its product throughout various geographic regions or it may want to have Market Specialization, in which different product ads could be broadcast in a single geographic location/country. Moreover, one can also take the approaches of Single Segment Concentration, Selective Specialization, or even Full Market Coverage very easily.

Companies such as Victoria's Secret, who are facing legal problems in displaying their ads in countries like Saudi Arabia, can easily choose not to broadcast the ads there with this tool. There is also a provision for Promoted Video Campaigns. The opportunities are immense for a Marketing Campaign. In the above portion, the targeting based on location is mentioned, but it also has an immense treasure of various marketing tools for marketers' ease. Demographic targeting allows an advertiser to target their audience based on their age, gender, or a combination of the two. Also, language targeting serves ads only to users who have selected to access the site in a certain language. Moreover, audiences could be targeted based on their interest. For example, if I am promoting a video of a new car, most likely I will put my video under the Auto Enthusiast or Sports Fan category. Now, with any individual who watches a video from these two categories, there is a high probability that my uploaded video will be suggested to the viewer based on the resemblance to the searched keyword or even on the basis of number of hits on my video. Sometimes, while signing up for an account, the user himself mentions the category of videos he would like to subscribe/view. It becomes all the easier for targeting if the user has already given that information.

A company can tactfully use its promotional videos in sites like YouTube, and if the sensation could be created among the users of the Internet, it could be a huge advertising success without spending even a penny. Old Spice has created a successful campaign through YouTube having the maximum number of subscriptions until November 2010 (YouTube, 2010). Other companies like Apple, Nike, Disney Parks, Microsoft, Sony, etc., have also created some very successful advertising campaigns through YouTube. Among the Sponsors category, Old Spice has the all-time maximum viewership of 160,483,371, followed by Sony Pictures having 76,772,340 viewers (YouTube, 2010). These are huge numbers. Commercial organizations will be longing to have such a viewership by its audience/prospective customers.

## Cookies Role in YouTube

Since the techniques of advertising are in discussion, the simple but effective concept of cookies could hardly be avoided. It's quite an old concept now, and most of the well-established companies with an online presence use this concept. It is a very effective and efficient way of providing customization and a useful tool for online service marketing in the Customer Relationship Module (CRM) domain. Actually, a cookie is nothing but a small text file that is being placed in the secondary memory of the user's computer. It is not a virus as a lot of people have a misconception about it. It simply collects the information about the websites visited by the user or the items selected/bought by the user or even records the category of the videos that are being watched most by the user. This information is then sent to the particular website which has put the cookie inside the user's computer. So, the next time the user opens the site, he/she is being greeted with customized items/displays or sometimes even with their own name without even being logged in. The cookies made the life of marketers really easy because the visitors of a site are being showed only those items that interest them. Nowadays, some advanced cookies are being created which replicate themselves in many locations in the memory that are difficult to delete. These cookies now work like a magic for the online marketers and are the virtual sales agent for the firms following the customer everywhere. These cookies are so powerful now that a site putting a cookie in the user's computer not only can customize products in its own site, but it haunts the viewer in every site he visits by displaying ads in the category he likes until, and unless, he is enticed to make the purchase/sign up for membership. From personal experience, I would like to quote that once I viewed a video for a nice pair of shoes on YouTube. Then afterwards, the ads of that shoe category started to follow me on whatever video I watched. Ultimately, it was so luring that I had to watch almost all the videos of that shoe category. These are the wonderful magic of cookies.

But the work of the marketing department does not end here. Putting a video in a social media like YouTube is very easy, but the main challenge is to properly maintain it focusing the target audience. Moreover, it is extremely necessary to form a dedicated team for the sole purpose of analyzing and keeping an eagle's eye view of all the videos concerned with the company. It may happen that competitors of certain brands may put some defaming videos against a brand to decrease its brand value. The Dominos Scandal video uploaded on YouTube is a good example of an employee trying to degrade an established brand. The video showed an employee putting nasal fluid in the pizza while making it. The company watchdogs should be extremely vigilant towards such incidents, and necessary and efficient corrective actions have to be taken immediately as an uploaded video is very difficult to remove. Once the image is lost, it's extremely difficult to regain the lost image.

Some other ways of advertising are also there on YouTube. Without just having to depend on a standalone video ad and waiting for viewers to click and view the ad, some new innovative ways have come up.

New formats have come up in the market such as:

- Click to Play

- Banner Ads

- In-Stream ads

## Click to Play

In these type of ads, the ad is not played until and unless the user clicks on the ad link being displayed beside another video. Here, if the user is not interested, he is not getting disturbed because the ad is not played unless he wishes to watch it. So, this video will only earn for you if the user clicks on the video link and then watches the video; otherwise, it will not generate any revenue for you at all. But still it is the most popular among all because one has to take care of the viewer also as it is his choice to watch the video or not.

## Banner Ads

These are the standard banner ads used on YouTube and very similar to any type of Internet advertising banner ads. These ads could even be played in the bottom part of the video being played. They are used as a separate video from the video that the viewer is viewing at that particular time.

## In-Stream advertisement

This is a very innovative way of showing advertisement. The company has to register for displaying such an advertisement. These ads are being displayed on the screen in the slack time when streaming of the video takes place. The format emerged as a result of the slow Internet connection in most parts of the world, especially in India due to poor broadband penetration. During the streaming time, the ad is played as the main video takes time to get streamed. This generates a lot of revenue if the Internet connection is slow as it will come effective only when the buffering of the video is too slow.

One of the most important benefits that YouTube provides for its users is that the companies can measure the viewership of their video ad campaigns with the help of the YouTube's Reporting Tool. It helps the company analyze the effectiveness of its campaign. So, a company is aware of what it should do in order to increase the viewers. If sufficient buzz is created, then it's well and good else some corrective measures have to be taken to increase the viewership. The results can be obtained in a proper easy-to-understand graphical format. Then the results are analyzed by the employees of that company and appropriate actions are performed on the basis of the results that have been received.

## A Real Life Story

The social media boom has also worked like magic for many small and new entrepreneurs. It has come as a dream come true for some of them. To quote specifically, Devesh Mishra, who is a cab driver from Varanasi, is making his livelihood based on social media, especially from YouTube. What happened was when he used to drive his cab in Rajasthan a few years back, a tourist from Switzerland used his taxi for travelling into the city and shot a video of the cab driver and uploaded it on YouTube. Since then, Devesh started to get many international bookings for his cab, especially from Switzerland as his video was seen by many citizens of Switzerland. So, instead of finding someone new to take a ride, they preferred him. Now, most of his bookings are done via social media much in advance. Like Mishra, several other entrepreneurs operating with shoestring budgets have figured out that social media is a great advertising tool to showcase their goods, talk to clients, build long-term relationships, and generally boost their businesses without spending a penny. So, YouTube has worked in favor of many people, and they are earning quite well from it.

*Andrew Mckinnon*

# Chapter 7
# Using Social Media to Promote Your Channel

The impact of social media on your YouTube subscriber and view count is of such tremendous importance that this entire chapter is dedicated to using social media successfully to your advantage.

The primary goal of using social media is only to increase your view count in your videos and develop a strong fan base that favors your videos. This doesn't directly give you any profits, but it helps build a solid viewer base and reaches out to those who do not know about you or your videos. In the end, it all comes down to your view count and ad clicks on your videos, which significantly affects your profit.

If used in the right way, social media can help boost your view count several fold. As mentioned before, your YouTube videos have their unique address or "URL." Copy this URL and paste it in your Facebook, Twitter, or any forums you frequent. Any user who clicks this URL will be directed to your YouTube video, at which point, if it interests the person, he will subscribe and add to your pool of views. Make sure to include these URLs only in places that do disturb or annoy the other users.

Try and convince your family and friends to see your videos beforehand when you start out. It is important to get someone's opinion as it may be different from yours. Try to correct your mistakes before using social media platforms to promote your videos and channel. If you end up uploading a mediocre video in your initial stages, your audience will get an impression of you being a mediocre video creator. Under no circumstances should this happen. So, take precautionary measures, and make your first few videos the best before promoting them.

Given below are some of the most widely used social media platforms to effectively promote your videos and channel.

Read on to know how you should go about promoting your videos and how you can gain a larger audience.

## Facebook

Facebook, as an example, is the perfect place to paste these URLs on your own timeline or on a Facebook page that you have created to promote your channel. This way, only people who are interested can view your videos. Unnecessarily posting URLs and videos on another user's page or private chats could take a turn for the worse as it builds a bad reputation. Facebook has the additional option of paid marketing. You pay a nominal price, and your videos will be displayed at the top of the user's homepage. This means more traffic as your videos have more chance of being watched if they are placed first. Despite nominal prices, you might not want to use this option initially until you have enough subscribers and a steady view count. Using YouTube for profit requires zero initial investment, and hence, you should be able to pay for the marketing from your profits and not your pockets.

Despite this, many viewers stop watching your videos after clicking on your link. To overcome this, link the URL of a playlist of your videos that are related in some way or the other instead of a single video. This helps the viewers get interested and stay interested.

## Instagram

Not many YouTube video creators consider using Instagram as a way to promote their videos, but it is an absolute fun and easy way to do so. As with Facebook and Twitter, you need to link your Instagram account as well on your YouTube channel and vice-versa. Instagram should be used to give regular updates about your life, if you want to of course. Most people like to know about the daily life of YouTubers, and you should get a good number of hits on your Instagram profile, which means you also have a chance at gaining more hits on your YouTube channel and videos. Apart from this, you can and should upload teasers of your next video. It should not contain the essence of the video itself; rather, you need to post pictures that make the audience hungry for more. This way, you are guaranteed a good number of views on your videos if you make your Instagram posts enigmatic. A good idea would be to release a teaser the day before you upload the actual video. This ensures your viewers are still interested. Setting up an

Instagram account is fairly easy, and you can update your posts on it regularly with just your smartphone, which saves a lot of time.

## Twitter

Twitter also holds great potential in increasing your view count. Hashtags are your greatest weapons; use them right, and you can easily set a trend that helps with promoting your video. Make sure to reach out to people with similar interests as you, and give them shootouts in your videos and request them to do the same for you. This ensures that their fans, subscribers, and viewers know about you, which once again spells nothing but profit.

Being interactive is one of the best ways to sustain the interests of your viewers, and Twitter chat is the best way to interact with your viewers. Create a custom hashtag, tell your viewers the exact date and time you will be online to chat, and start chatting! Interact with your viewers, respond to questions, figure out what they expect more from you, build some trust, and lastly, always thank them for spending their precious time to view your videos. This not only helps create more interest, but also a higher number of viewers as everybody likes their opinion being considered. This can sound slightly arduous and time consuming, but Twitter is very smartphone-friendly. You can perform these actions while travelling or when you have free time, saving you time that can be used to create content for your next video or to go about your daily life.

While Facebook should be the primary platform through which you get the support of viewers, you should aim to provide regular updates on the topic of the next video via Twitter. Note that your tweet is limited to 140 characters, so it only makes sense to keep your updates as short and mysterious as possible to provoke the interests of your viewers. Always link URLs to your videos at the end of your Facebook post or Twitter tweet.

## Blogs

If you are a blogger with an already well-established audience, promoting your YouTube channel should be much easier. Simply include URLs to your blog on your YouTube channels and to your YouTube channel in your blog. This leads to more traffic in both places and hence more income. Creating videos related to the article you blogged about and pasting their URLs in your article is the best way to increase traffic. A video demonstration or tutorial or summary is always preferred to a written one. A blog requires you to regularly update the content; else it loses the interest of viewers. This gives an incentive to update your YouTube videos and stay ahead of others in trending topics to tremendously support your blog and vice-versa.

If you are not interested in creating a blog and maintaining it or feel that it takes up too much of your time, then it is a good idea to look up bloggers who create similar content to your videos. You can then request them to link your videos or your channel in their blogs for a small fee (only if the blogger has a large fan base, of course) or you could strike a deal where you link their blogs in your videos and they link your videos in their blogs. This is a great way to set up mutual trust and gain each other's followers.

## Google+

YouTube is owned by Google, so why not use Google's own social media platform, Google+, to promote your channel? The great thing about Google+ is that you don't have a character limit like Twitter does. It is a great replacement to blogging, and you should consider it as a miniature blogging platform. All you need to do is create your own personal logo, a custom look on the channel, and give your Google+ page a personal touch to let yourself be more easily recognizable. You can include your video links in your posts to gain more support. Unlike Facebook, a large number of Google+ users use it for marketing. You should try to find out similar individuals or professionals in the same niche and engage with them. Try to share their posts if you feel the need to do so, and you increase your chances of them sharing your content. It is also a great place to get feedback and advice from professionals who have already been down the road you are taking. Like Twitter, hashtags are used in Google+ as well but just not to the same extent. Use precise hashtags to get more hits and never give your posts innumerable inaccurate hashtags as it is an indisputable way of bringing forth hate comments from your audience.

## MySpace

MySpace is another popular social networking website and can be used extensively to promote your YouTube channel.

How to use MySpace in this aspect will be covered in detail with explicit instructions in a later chapter.

## The Share Trend

Sharing is an amazing way to rally more viewers. All it requires is you to ask your viewers to share your videos if they liked it with their friends and family. It is a given that most of them won't. But once a few people start sharing and your videos get around, it's only a matter of time before it is trending.

The idea behind sharing is to get you introduced to people who do not know about your videos yet. They view your videos and, in turn, share them, which leads to a hopefully never-ending cycle. Shares are the best way to get your videos around. What this means is your videos gain more traffic.

A requirement to this is a lenient privacy setting on your social media pages like Facebook and Twitter. You *want* your videos to be watched by people other than your friends. Make sure your videos are visible to the public at large, and you have a shot at gaining the large number of viewers that you want. Keeping your settings secured eventually will lead to a loss in your subscriber count as your videos will not be going around the social media platform as much as you would like them to. For this reason, it is optimal to create a different account or a page in the social media platform dedicated only to your videos. You can link back to your personal profile which you will be keeping secure and tell your viewers to personally give you requests and feedback or so there. This helps with security as well as getting you the maximum shares possible.

Social media is all about a person's opinion being heard. You may upload videos and promote them with all your resources, and they will not generate the expected traffic if you do not take some time to respond to your viewers. This is the most important part of using social media to promote videos. Always remember to ask people to like, subscribe, and comment. This will give you a general feedback. Ignore the mean posts if they do not have any constructive criticism. A good idea would be to upload a "Q & A" video where you answer some of the questions asked in your previously uploaded videos. This serves a dual role of making your viewers feel appreciated and increasing your income.

Effectively utilizing the social media available to you almost guarantees in gaining never-before-seen traffic and subscribers. It also ensures you have active and not passive subscribers, i.e., those who subscribe to you and view your videos regularly.

*Andrew Mckinnon*

# Chapter 8
# Ads for Monetizing On YouTube

One of the most common methods of earning on YouTube is through advertisements. Read on to learn how:

First, set up a channel and upload videos with genuine content, which will lure in more viewers.

Then decide if you want to add advertisements and monetize on your channel through them. The ads can be run on your video or even beside it.

There are different types of ads to choose from. The ad could play before your video starts running or somewhere in the middle of it. You could also allow the ad to run alongside your content at the side. You can also choose whether the ad can be skipped or has to be played throughout before your content is displayed. Different options will generate different revenue for you. A banner ad will generate less income than a TrueView ad.

Once you decide all this, open an AdSense account for your channel. This will help YouTube to make the transactions when payday comes.

Your video is optimized for running ads once you enable them to be run with all the videos on your channel. This ad viewership is then used to monetize your account.

You can increase your audience with the help of earned views. Using AdWords can help you access audience suited for your content according to their choice. AdSense has been used by many ventures to increase their income. The investment is quite minimal while proper use can generate a lot of income. If the advertisements are really good and the webmasters put in maximal effort, the income can be quite good. Effective traffic generation, valuable content, and the right text can all help in this.

The ad for your video appears in another and can be opened if the viewer clicks on it. You pay for this click. The viewer then watches the video with ads enabled on your video by other content creators. This is what you are paid for. A percentage of the revenue from this is given to you. Thus, you can use AdWords for your videos and allow others to advertise on them in order to earn some money.

## AdSense and AdWords

### *What is AdSense?*

AdSense is software that should be placed on a website in order to generate income. It automatically plays an ad on the website, and if a person clicks on it, then the website earns money. All sites that generate a lot of views should use AdSense. It is essential to use it on those websites that experience a lot of clicks on a daily basis. So, it is a great idea to add it to your YouTube account. If you have a lot of subscribers, then it is essential that you link the two and generate an income from it.

### *How does it work?*

It is simple. Once you link it, an ad will automatically start to play before your video starts. If it is a big ad, then an option of skipping it will appear at the bottom, but if it is a small ad, then it won't give the option. The idea is for people to like the product in the ad and click on it. Once they do, they will be redirected to the product's website. This is based on chance as not all people will be interested in clicking on ads that appear on the website. However, if the right type of ad plays, then the uploader will get paid for it.

### What is AdWords?

AdWords is software, which helps in generating revenue per click on the ad. It is used to earn an income, and if the person clicks on an ad, then the uploader receives money for it. It is based on the concept of a word that is typed in the search box. Say, for example, somebody typed in "lady." Then your ad corresponding to "lady" will be placed on the right top corner. If the person clicks on it, then he or she will help you earn money. But they have to click and not just see it in order for you to earn an income.

### How much do you earn?

That is hard to say. It depends on the number of people that visit your site. If you have a lot of subscribers, then chances are at least 2/3rds of them will click on the ads. But that is just a rough estimate. Although you get paid very little per click, it is still a good idea to make use of it.

You will possibly make a lot of money on a monthly basis. It is estimated that most people who have 200,000 plus subscribers can make between $20 and $50 a day. This is a great number considering it is passive income and getting generated without you having to actively take part in it. You will be able to supplement your monthly income and set yourself up with a great source of income, which will come in handy when you retire.

### When are you paid?

Google generally pays you after 30 days of you reaching a $100 in your account. So, you have to wait till it reaches $100, and there is no way that you can encash when you have any less money. When someone clicks on the ad, then you get to keep 55% of it and Google gets 45%. Many people have questioned this, but you are getting the opportunity to make the money thanks to Google. So, it is fair that they get a part in it.

### Is it all-automatic?

Yes. It is automatic. Once you place AdSense on your website, you don't have to do anything except wait for the ads to play and get the money into your account. So, once you are all set up, you don't have to do much for it. You will keep receiving your money on a daily basis.

### Is there a format?

Yes. There are many formats that you can choose from. You can place up to three ads on your page at any one time. You can choose the format you like. You have the chance to choose the dimensions of the ads and make it look as aesthetic as possible. You can place a few ads and see if it is looking nice and then go ahead with it. Nothing is final until you give it a go ahead. Remember that the ads placed above the fold do well compared to the ads that are placed below the fold. This is because there is the chance the person looking at the ads will not go below the fold at all.

### How will AdSense know what ads to play?

When you sign up with AdSense, you will have to mention the details of your website. AdSense will go through it and look at the key words that are present in it. Then, they will direct ads that have the specific keyword in it. So, every time someone hits them, the ads will appear.

### Should I have a specific account?

Yes. You have to sign up with AdSense. It is a fairly simple process, and you only have to fill out a form for it. Once you do, you will have the chance to link it to your website. From there on, everything is automatic. There are some people who will simply sign up, but there is no sense in that. There is no point in signing up with it if you don't have a big following online.

### Are there any restrictions?

Yes. There are a few restrictions when it comes to using AdSense. For example, it is important to not click on your own ads as that won't make any sense. You have to let others make money for you, and if you are clicking on your own ads, then what is the point? It is like sabotaging the plan, and it will not go down too well with AdSense. In fact, it is a very strict rule to not click on your own ads. AdSense will check your clicks per month, and if they see that many clicks have come from you or even a few of them have come from your IP address, then they will not think twice before blocking you. Similarly, it is a strict rule to not place ads in your emails. You have to strictly place it only on your websites which attract a lot of clicks. This being your YouTube account in this case.

### *TrueView Ad Format?*

TrueView is an ad format that you can select in which the viewer has the choice of watching the ad or skipping it if felt unnecessary. Ironically, 8 out of 10 people *do* watch the ad until the end even with the option of skipping the ad, but only if the skip button is included. This can only work to your benefit for you will be paid based on the number of views on clicks in the ad in your video. This also benefits the sponsors (you can also be one to promote your own channel) because they need to pay only for ads that are viewed. The additional option of skipping the ad makes sure the sponsor attracts only those who are truly interested about their product or service, and hence they do not mind paying the fee to have their ads displayed. This is a complete win-win situation and is absolutely recommended over the "overlay-in-video ad" format.

## CPM and RPM

Now that you know how to use AdSense and AdWords effectively, it is important for you to know how your income is generated. This is where the terms "CPM" and "RPM" come into the picture.

CPM, standing for Cost Per Mile, is a term used by advertisers who want to place ads in your videos. It is essentially the cost they pay per every thousand views of your video. Video creators, however, should want to know more about RPM, which is the revenue you earn per the thousand views. You may see the term "eCPM" on your YouTube channel, which shows your earnings. It's the effective CPM of your videos. It is important to note that this is your earnings *before* YouTube takes its cut. Your actual revenue will be less than this amount. But with over 100,000 views per video, you approximately make $200, give or take a few dollars. This is where RPM comes into play. You can calculate your revenue per thousand views by simple math after YouTube has taken its cut.

### Is it the number of views that increases my earnings?

This is an important and widely asked question. No, it is not your views that pay you; it is the ads that you display on your video. There are two types of ads; one that offers to pay you "per view" and one that offers to pay you "per click.". When the advertiser says "per view," what they mean is that at least half the ad was viewed before being skipped. You do not get paid if they skip the ad after the minimum time of five seconds required before the "Skip:" option appears. This is where CPM comes into play.

However, when the advertiser pays "per click," the viewer has to click the ad for you to get any revenue from it. There are no exceptions to this, and it is a give-in that pay-per-view ads give you more revenue than pay-per-click ads. Ironically, adding the "Skip Ad" button is better for you, as stated previously, and the sponsor because only those interested in the product or service actually click the link. The sponsor pays only when the ad has been clicked, so it is a definite way of getting interested customers hooked onto their product rather than paying for people who just want to browse.

These form some of the basic FAQs that get asked on the subject, and I hope I have answered yours successfully.

# Chapter 9

# Tips for Using YouTube for Business

As long as you go about it the right way, YouTube can really help you in business. Use the following tips:

1. Give it time. Don't expect instant results when you start using YouTube. Focus on getting the best content on your channel, and with patience, you will see the growth. Abandoning your efforts in a short while would be completely fruitless and expecting super fast profits is impractical. Think of it as a plant that you are trying to nurture. Is it possible for a plant to come up within a few days? Of course not! Think of your channel as a seed and only by nurturing it will you have the chance to help it grow in size and volume. But you have to remain consistent and not take your channel for granted once it gains traction.

You have to nurture it and make sure that it blossoms into a big tree.

2. As you start out, it would benefit you to collaborate with a user who is already established. This way, you can benefit from their experience and also pull in their audience for yourself. You can pay them to endorse you on their channel through videos or by sharing links in their section. Just go through the channels listed on YouTube and find ones which are similar to yours with a lot of subscriptions. Ideally, a channel with at least a couple of hundred thousand would be a good place to start. You can even exchange the favor and promote them on your channel if they want. This link would help to validate your YouTube existence further. But make sure it is someone who has a good number of subscribers and not just a few. You might end up paying them and not get any subscribers yourself. There are some who have a staggering number of subscribers, and you can choose them as they won't mind sharing a few of theirs with others. Again, work out all the terms and conditions before you get into a legal agreement with someone lest you have to deal with unwanted problems later on.

3. Customize your channel and give it a personal touch. Add branding and other specific details that will make your channel unique and attractive as well. This helps to highlight your channel and all its content. There are many ways in which you can customize your channel, and you can choose a theme that works well with the type of videos you have to offer. Remember, if you have a nice page, then people will take a liking to it and subscribe to your channel.

4. If you are making an advertisement video, you need to make it engaging. It is not just about showing your product or service but about convincing the viewer to buy it. The ad should help the viewer to feel engaged and interested in the product. Make the video creative and alluring for the viewer but not so long that they don't make it to the end of the video. You have to try and make it as interesting and fun as possible as nobody likes boring videos that are not intriguing. Look at other videos like yours and take a few tips. However, do not copy anything from someone else's advertisement videos.

5. Use all the features on YouTube to your maximum benefit. For instance, utilize the caption features for videos. This helps in making your video more accessible to hearing

impaired people and also to those speaking other languages. This simple feature instantly increases your otherwise limited audience. If they can't understand what is being said, the viewer is hardly about to watch it. If you are not sure where these are or how to use them, then you can simply YouTube it! That's right, there will be hundreds of videos out there that will explain to you these features and get you to use them to your benefit.

6. Using real people in your advertisements has amazing benefits. The viewer feels that the product or service is more authentic and relates to the story narrated in the ad. Finding a face for your business can work to your benefit. Have a good mix of all races to appeal to many people. Don't stick to just pretty faces and get real people to pose, similar to what Dove does in their advertisement campaigns. They get real people to pose as opposed to models. If your audience connects with reality, then you have to serve them just that.

7. Keep interacting with the subscribers of your channel. The comments section is meant for this and helps you to create a better bond with your viewers. This makes your presence more real and the viewer more likely to keep

subscribed if you respond to them. You must have seen how many times there will be a lot of interested people wanting to talk, but the uploader will not be available to comment. Even if you churn out several videos a day, it is important to interact with your audience and understand what they are looking for. You have to give them what they want in order to hold on to them. If you don't interact with them or are easily offended by a few comments, then it is useless. If you wish to make it big, then you have to jump in with your audience to get to know them better and increase your reach.

8.   Make your channel user friendly. Create playlists to make things simpler and more specifically suited to the subscribers' taste. Just listing them all together can be a little tiresome for the viewer who might be looking for something in particular. So, you have to know what needs to be placed where in order to help people with their searching and sorting. Would you like it if you were given a raw list where everything is scattered around? Similarly, you need to sort and arrange the videos in such a way that you have the chance to pander to even the picky audiences.

9.  Use links to somehow drive the viewers from YouTube to your main website. Let the links pop up in the middle of your video or in the description section. Or you could even add the link every time you post on the comment section as well. This will help in generating more views to your own website instead of keeping them confined to your YouTube channel. But don't bombard them with these links and annoy them. You have to know where and when to notify someone about it. If you are trying too hard, then it might come across as being desperate for attention. So, try and keep it simple.

10. Use relevant tags for your videos and give them some good thought. This will help your video to pop up on their search if you use the right ones. There is a list available with Google that lists out the most popular tags in some of the highest search topics. You can go through that list and find the words that can be tagged in order to help your videos appear on top of the list. Apart from those, pick out words that you would type in if you were looking for a video like the one you have uploaded. There are a lot of options to choose from, so you can use words, which will direct your targeted audience to your video.

11. Use Google AdWords to get paid views. Once you use this, make sure that the beginning of your ad is especially engaging in order to keep the viewer watching the rest. This way it gets counted as a view.

12. Try to engage your viewers even after the video has run its course. End by telling them to do something on your website, comment below, or anything that keeps them on for longer and might benefit you.

13. You should also promote your channel or videos on other platforms. This creates a larger audience for you. Many websites allow you to embed the URL for YouTube videos on their page. Utilize this to direct people from other platforms to your channel. Be on the lookout for these platforms and make the best of what they have to offer for you. You have to try and promote yourself as much as possible and make use of all the opportunities that are presented to you. Don't get stuck wondering if it is right for you to do this or if it is right for you to do that. As long as it is benefitting you, there is no right or wrong. Just do it and expand your horizons.

14. Be active on your channel. Neglecting it and being inactive might even cause your subscribers to unsubscribe. Once you log back in, it would then be like starting all over again. An up-to-date channel will engage more people in it and thus increase your viewers. So, if you are busy with something, then ask someone else to update it. Keep the videos coming in consistently in order to keep your audiences entertained and get more and more people to subscribe to your channel.

15. Google analytics can be used to keep track of the performance of your channel. Use this to do a study and see where you're going, right or wrong. It is not enough to check whether you are headed in the right direction. You have to fix it if you are going wrong and stick to a plan if you are going right.

16. If you are promoting a particular product, you can make a how-to video to make it simpler for the viewer to use it if they make a purchase. If they view the video prior to buying the product, convince them that it is easy to use and worth the money. Don't use technical terms, and keep it as simple as possible. It is important to demonstrate

something to your audience in a simple way and get them to buy your product.

17. Create contests or events on your channels to engage more participation from your viewers and keep them involved. If you successfully garner a large subscriber base and are killing it with the ads, then you surely can afford to diversify into merchandise and give your audience that extra something to connect with you in a better way. You can also organize regular contests to give away cool stuff, and there is nothing like a celebrity-endorsed mug or t-shirt to get your subscribers all excited.

18. Keep going. Never give up on what you are doing. Even if you have a few subscribers now, the numbers are bound to increase with time. There is no point in giving up on something that you started with a lot of enthusiasm. So, don't give up on your YouTube endeavors and keep going until you succeed. Just because it is a passive source of income doesn't mean that you take it casually. You have to take it up with equal enthusiasm and see to it that you turn it into a success.

19. Good network of friends. Remember to always have a good network of friends who have a big presence. You need all the help you can get to promote your channel, and if you have friends who are willing to help you out, then there is nothing better. You have to ask them to share your links on their websites, blogs, Facebook pages, etc. It is always good to have a large network when you wish to make it big online. If you have one yourself and have a lot of friends on Facebook, then it is best to get them to subscribe to your channel and ask them to ask their friends to do so as well.

20. Tie ups with bloggers. Get acquainted with all the best bloggers in your area or country. It pays to be in the good books of people who are already established. Even if you have a tie up with a successful YouTube blogger, you have to promote your content outside of YouTube as well. For this, you need the help of bloggers who are quite popular. If they put in links to your YouTube channel, then imagine how many subscribers you can attract with ease. Even if they ask you for a fee to promote you, then it is well worth it given how many subscribers you can earn with ease.

21. Uniqueness. Remember that being unique is your biggest USP. You will make it big based on how unique you

really are. If you choose to do what others are doing, then it is useless. You have to choose an offbeat path and do things that will catch people's attention. Be as unique and different as possible to make the most of your YouTube channel.

22. Protect it. It pays to watermark your content in some way or the other. This is extremely important as there are many people out there who will copy from you and get away with it. Even if you find out some time later about it, they would have successfully used it not to your advantage, and so prevention is better than cure. Try and copyright what you have and add in enough watermarks to protect your content from thieves. Make sure the watermark is visible and cannot be easily edited out. Have a consistent watermark and don't change it up every now and then. Make it your identification mark and try and choose something that makes sense to you.

23. Calls to action. Never forget to add in calls to action. This means that you tell your audience to subscribe to your channel or like or leave a comment. Many times, people don't realize that all this is an important part of video watching on YouTube. You have to remind them to do this

and also ask them to leave you feedback to voice their opinion on the videos. You have to tell them that this is important as you need to provide them with more content and keep the channel going.

24. Summarize. Always remember to summarize the video either at the end or at the beginning. This is important because you have to remind people what the video was all about. It is especially needed for long videos. So, if you added in something important at the beginning of the video, then you need to add it again at the end or remind people about it. This is especially needed for long videos that surpass the 15-minute mark. But keep the summary short and simple. Don't add in too many things and make it boring.

25. Editing. Never forget to edit out unwanted bits from your videos. There is no point in letting those remain there, and you have to get rid of them to shorten the video and allow people to see only what is needed and important. If you are having trouble understanding what needs to be edited out, then you can ask a friend to help you. Show him or her the video and ask for their opinion to help you out. There are also online tools available that will help you

assess what needs to remain and what can be cut out. Once you are done with it, show it to a test audience again to make sure that it is good enough to be uploaded on to your channel.

## Mistakes to avoid when choosing YouTube as a source of passive income

### *Never copy*

This is the first mistake to avoid. Many times, we feel just so inspired by something that we see on the Internet that we decide to emulate it. This is not a bad idea if you are planning to do it for your own satisfaction, but if you are doing it to upload it on YouTube and monetize from it, then it is a bad idea. There are so many copycats doing the rounds, and nobody subscribes to them. So, you can take something as an inspiration and model your video or videos around it but trying to do the same thing is not worthy, and you might have your videos pulled down for being a duplicate.

### Don't steal

Remember, copying is one thing; stealing is another. Even if you copy something, it is still like your creation, but if you steal something, then that is illegal. Don't get into trouble for copying or stealing something from someone else be it a video, music, pictures, or anything else. It is vital that you remain as free from trouble as possible. There are many who will purposely copy and try and amass a big crowd before their video gets pulled down. But continuing on with this trend will not work out in the long run. You have to do whatever is legal and not copy and steal stuff just to try and amass a large audience. If your content is really good and 100% original, then you will definitely make it big in this business.

### Don't make it boring and long

People will hate anything that is long and boring. There is no point in creating long videos that are just at the 15-minute mark. Tame it and make it shorter. Keep it as interesting as possible. If you are demonstrating a recipe then try and minimize the time taken to assemble things and have everything ready to be used. Similarly, don't have a lot of voids in your video. It has to be interesting every second, and you must not add in anything that will distract your audience or bore them.

### Stop if it isn't working

Many people can't wrap their head around the fact that something is not working for them. That can happen to those who have a great content to offer, and yet it has not clicked. Give it another shot and try and promote it on better forums. If it clicks, it clicks; if it doesn't, then don't get hung over it. You need to move on and that is possible only if you accept the fact that something is not going right and you need to move on. If you waste time with something that is not working, then it will eat away into your productive time. So, try and let go of videos that are not working and concentrate on the ones that really are.

### Don't forget subscribe

Never forget to add the subscribe button. There are many times when you will be so busy and so excited to see your videos on YouTube that you will forget to add the subscribe button. Now that is not something you want happening to you after all the effort that you put in it. So, be as alert as possible and avoid rookie mistakes. You have to check everything on your page and make sure that everything is in its place. If at any time you wonder why you are not having very many subscribers, check if you have included the button in the first place.

### Add End-Cards

Sometimes, the viewer just won't get motivated to click the Subscribe button that is located below the video. Taking into account these cases, creating an end-card with a link on screen to subscribe to you would be in your best interest. Not only do end-cards give a custom flourish to your video, they also coax the user into subscribing to you. Your audience would feel compelled to click the link on the video. Apart from just adding a link for subscription, you could add links to related videos and playlists to get the extra views. It is not mandatory, but adding end-cards do help in the long run and make it much easier to get more subscribers.

### Always turn on Skip Ads

As contradictory as it may sound, this is a great idea to keep your viewers interested in your videos and your income passively growing. If a person does not want to view an ad, he or she should have the right to not do so. You may be of the opinion that you gain more income as more people view the ads. This is not true. If you have turned off the Skip Ads option on your channel for your videos, you are only going to lose your subscribers. Turn it on, and give the viewers the chance to decide. This helps in gaining a larger viewer base in the long run.

It is a statistical fact that over 60% of the viewers actually *do* watch the ads even when the Skip Ad button is included. It may not sound like much, but when a view count of 100,000 is considered for one particular video, it earns you approximately $150 to $200 a month. Now, this is just one video with a 100,000 views. When you have quite a few videos uploaded, it is not just your latest video that helps you earn more. Your previous videos will be getting views just at a slightly slower pace. But it does add up with your current videos. Now, imagine your content going viral with a positive response and gaining over a million views. This is where you start making your big bucks.

### Allow comments

Many people fear the comments that they will receive from people. You have to understand that your customer's comments are extremely important. You have to allow comments and not disable them. Even if there will be bad ones and mean people saying ugly things, you cannot allow it to affect you. You have to allow them in order to understand how people perceive your videos. You have to skim through the comments and look at only the positive ones during the first few days of uploading videos just to remain confident. Once you are strong enough, you can look at the negatives as well and work on them to better your own channel. So, don't disable the comments and allow them on your videos.

### Keep Descriptions Interesting

Most viewers hit the "Back" button if you don't have a description, because it is mostly people without interest who keep their descriptions empty. Keep it lengthy, keep it innovative, and most importantly, keep it as descriptive as possible. The need for the lengthy description is stated in a previous chapter. The viewer must be itching to watch the video by the time he or she reaches the end of the description. You can also link all your social media platforms at the end of the description.

### Don't bash people

It is easy to get carried away and start bashing those who have left behind bad comments. But if you do so, then you will probably lose the subscribers that you have. The idea is to allow people to say what they want. If someone is being obscene, then simply ignore them. The more attention you pay to them, the more confidence that they develop. So, allow them to say what they want, and you do your job. If the bashing is getting too much, then you can flag them, and they will be kicked out for good.

### Don't follow the herd

This is a golden rule when it comes to making it big on YouTube. If you follow what everyone else is doing, then you will never succeed. It is important to set your own trends. What use is it if you follow someone else and do something that they are doing? You will have to compete with them, which is not worth your time or effort. It is fine to follow someone in a broader category but to narrow it down to doing the same thing as them is stupid. Say, for example, it is fine to take up recipes as your forte but demonstrating the same recipe as someone else is useless. You have to come up with your own unique creations and something traditional so that people take a liking to it.

### Don't be impatient

Never be impatient when it comes to making it big. You have to have a lot of patience and, more important, confidence in order to make your channel a success. Don't expect to see overnight results unless you have made a spectacular video that is bound to go viral. Try and remain positive and know that people will like your videos ultimately but need a little time to subscribe to you.

### Be reasonable

Be reasonable in your expectations. Don't aim too high at the very beginning. Understand that it will take some time for people to get acquainted with your work and like it. You might get 100 subscribers a day, which is not bad considering you will get 360,000 a year. That is enough for you to get noticed by companies to tie up with you. Remember that passive income is a cumulative job, and you have to be patient and do all the right things in order to make it big.

## Always track

Many people don't track the traffic on their site and have no idea as to how many people are visiting their page. For this, it is important to track the number of people that visit and those who are clicking on ads, etc. Having basic knowledge is extremely important and you must track your YouTube page in order to know if a majority of the visitors are turning into your subscribers.

These are the major problems that you need to avoid when you choose to earn your passive income through YouTube.

*Andrew Mckinnon*

# Chapter 10

# Maintaining Your Viewership

The previous chapter dealt with a few mistakes to avoid. Even if you do unfortunately end up making mistakes, it is not too hard to set yourself straight and start over once again the right way. Once you start gaining a steady stream of views on your videos with favorable response, it is completely up to you to maintain the quality of your videos lest you lose your reputation. As difficult as it is to get a good viewer base, it is even more difficult to keep it growing (keyword here being difficult and not impossible).

Needless to say, the better your reputation as a good-quality video maker, the more views you get. You have built your channel now, created a solid viewer base, gained their trust, and are regularly posting fresh content much to your viewers' satisfaction. Here is when you need to be careful with each and every action you take. A small error is all it takes to tear down your reputation permanently and stop getting views altogether. Always remember, it's easier to ruin something than it is to preserve and nurture it. Here are some things you should and should not do to make sure you maintain the benchmark that you have set for yourself to keep your viewers happy, temporarily satisfied, and always hungry for more.

## Never Pester Viewers

This is possibly the worst thing you could do. Never pester your viewers to watch a particular new video that you have uploaded. You have provided an URL to your video; whether the person clicks the link or not is up to them and not you. Forcing people through private chats or spam posts leads to an almost instantaneous bad reputation, which you can never grow out of, especially in social media. It is comparatively easier for a person to "unsubscribe" or stop following you on various social media platforms than it is for you to gain their interest and trust. Never play with the viewers' trust.

## Never Belittle Other Creators

This goes without saying, but a large number of your subscribers may be the other creator's subscribers as well. You may have uploaded a video criticizing someone else, but the viewers may not see it from your point of view. Chances are you are going to permanently lose a few subscribers and views. Always request the other creator if you can include his name in your spoofs or gags before actually doing so. It can save you a lot of trouble in the long run with trying to get back your subscribers.

## Do Not Abuse Social Media

Linking your channel and videos in your updates is a good thing to do and is recommended, but posting the link on each comment or tweet you make is taking it too far. The key idea here is to make the viewers think you need their support, but you are not desperate for it. Showing desperation via social media creates an aversion towards you that you do not want to have. Never pester your friends or family to "share" your latest videos. It only creates a bad reputation.

## Stick to One Type of Content

It is important to stick to the one type of content you wish to create. It also helps in gain views when your viewers know that you are going to upload a video that is right up their niche. If you start creating videos with different ideas, you may lose the interest of those who want to see videos that you had made before. Always give an update about the next video in all your social media platforms. Once you feel that you can no longer be creative in one particular field, it is time to switch. Always give your viewers a heads-up about why you decided to make a new series of videos with no relation to the previous ones whatsoever. This way, you gain your viewers trust and respect, eventually raking in more viewers for your new videos.

## Strictly Follow a Schedule

Most YouTubers upload videos when they see fit on any day of the week. This is wrong. You need to maintain a schedule and religiously stick to it. There should be no procrastination here. Sticking to a particular day or two of the week lets everybody know that you will be uploading a new video on that day. This helps in gaining most of the views, especially from your subscribers, as they get notified of your videos first.

Let's take an example here. Assume you upload videos once a week, but you don't have a strict schedule. Your subscribers will know you have uploaded the video because they get alerted by email, but they might not have time to watch it as soon as it is released, and your regular visitors will not even know that you have a new video up and running. Once a day or two passes, they lose interest, and you lose your revenue. Now assume you upload videos strictly during mornings on Sundays. Your viewers will know that you will upload a video the next day and will be ready to watch it as soon as it is online. This helps create a good reputation with the viewers. It is also better for a person to tell his friends to "check this person's videos out on Sundays, it's the best" than it is to say, "The videos are good, but I never know when they get released."

## Place Ads Only at The Beginning

The importance of this cannot be stressed enough. It would be in your best interest to place your ads in the beginning and opt for a TrueView ad format. Keeping ads that cannot be skipped in the middle of your videos (called in-stream ads) irritates the viewers to the point where they may stop watching your video or may even unsubscribe. Consider the pros and cons of using in-stream ads instead of TrueView. Viewers must watch 15-30 seconds of the ad before being able to continue your video. If you have confidence in your content being interesting enough to your viewers, then in-stream ads make more than TrueView, as it *must* be watched. TrueView allows you to give your viewers the choice, which is heavily recommended, when you have short videos (3-5 minutes) as the viewer will definitely not want to waste 15-30 seconds in the middle of a short video.

## Never Fret Over Subscriber Count

This may sound strange, but your primary focus should *not* be on gaining subscribers, it should be to gain *more views*. Telling viewers that you do not have enough subscribers yet and will not upload a video until so-and-so number of subscribers is reached is not advisable. Hosting a giveaway or creating a contest once you do hit a certain level of subscriber count is recommended and helps make your viewers feel appreciated. Understand that subscribers are not a bad thing to have; in fact, subscribers are the ones who get news of your latest video first and can be the best way to get your video around initially. But the fact is that there is no guarantee that a subscriber will watch your video. There are a few who subscribe only to leave "hate" comments on your video or worse, your channel (and they don't even count as a view!). What matters to a small extent is active, loyal subscribers and, to a great extent, people who watch "related videos." This is where most of your views are going to be coming from. People are more likely to click on a related video than they are to type out what they want in the search bar. In the end, what matters is your viewer count and fan base and never the number of subscribers. It is a known fact that most of your subscribers will be passive.

These ideas may seem obvious at first glance, but it is very easy to do the wrong thing unintentionally. Always stay alert and be smart with your actions and you should be able to maintain your viewer base fairly well. Once you are confident that you will get a certain number of views on every video you upload, it is time to try to go one step higher and increase your view count. This is easy if you keep updating with fresh and trending ideas. All this eventually spells out only one thing - you start earning more, passively, without too much physical work. What supplemented your primary income can now potentially *turn into your primary income.*

## Use Annotations to Link

This is a neat trick to get your first-time viewers to watch your previously uploaded videos. Whenever your video contains something of relevance that you have discussed in one of your previous videos, include a small annotation at the bottom of the video with a link to that video. If the viewer has annotations switched off, he will not be able to see it, but it helps in the long run as most YouTubers have annotations turned on so as to not miss any important updates. You can also use annotations to correct yourself if you have made slight mistakes while recording the video. If you decide to not go with end-cards, then having an annotation that links to subscribing to you would be an optimal choice. Include this annotation at the end of the video where you call the viewers to action; that is, you ask them to like, subscribe, and share.

## Allow Embedding

When you get the choice of allowing embedding or not, allow it. Embedding is different from sharing wherein the viewer puts up the link in his blog or social media platform and clicking on it will lead to your YouTube video in the official YouTube website. Embedding allows the user to post the entire video itself in his blog or social media platform, where people can directly watch your video without having to move to a separate website to do so. Embedded videos are a great way to get your name around the embedder's social circle, drawing in more traffic. People are more motivated to click on a video and watch it rather than clicking on a link that has been shared and moving to another website to do the same thing. You will have lesser number of subscribers via embedding than you will via sharing as people will not be able to subscribe to your videos from another person's blog or website, but as stated earlier, it is never your subscriber count that matters, it is the number of views you video manages to get. This increases the chances of the ads you have on your video being watched, which is your source of income.

It is obviously not possible for everyone to become popular and a YouTube sensation despite putting your maximum efforts. Besides pure effort, it also requires a little luck. In the unfortunate case that it does not work out for you, it is time to see where you went wrong and try and correct yourself.

# Chapter 11

# Things to Do If You Fail

It is obvious that you will not always experience positive results when you decide to take up YouTube as a platform to earn your passive income. You will have to deal with bad situations and try and remain positive through it. Here are some things you can do if it is not working out for you.

## Restart

If you think it is not working out for you at all, then give it another shot. For that, you will have to stop what you are currently doing and start from scratch. Rethink it and re-strategize. Remember that you need to pay just as much attention to your passive income as you would to your active income. Chances are you are not paying enough attention to your account, and that is why it is not prospering. In any case, don't hold on to something that is not working for you and decide to restart. Delete everything or make a new account for yourself. If you believe in it, then you can choose a name for your channel that you think will be lucky.

## Research

Do your research. You have to do your research to come up with good content. For this, look at what others are doing and take cues from what they are getting right. Compare it with what you were doing and see if you were doing anything differently. Many times, there will not be big differences, and you have to look for smaller ones. The smaller ones will always have a big impact on the other person's overall performance. Say, for example, both of you do unboxing. Both open the box, describe it, and give reviews. But maybe the other person is switching on the device and demonstrating it for his or her audience, and you are not doing that because it is just an unboxing video. So, if you incorporate that into yours, then you will have the chance to increase your audience base.

## Use YouTube Analytics

You should occasionally use YouTube analytics to check your progress and see if your views actually have a positive transition, and if they don't, try to switch ad formats, as they can be the reason for ending up with less views. In case you have never used YouTube Analytics, and your attempt at promoting has failed, it is perfect time to start. YouTube Analytics shows you how well your viewership is turning out and indirectly tells you if your ads, annotations, and content have the positive effect you want them to. Once you get a basic idea of when you went wrong, start over again.

## Ask

It is always a good idea to approach someone who is doing well on YouTube. Some can be friendly and some won't. You have to choose someone who will share the knowledge with you. Approach someone who has good reviews and a lot of subscribers and ask them how they made it big. Similarly, read stories about people who have made it big in the business. You can find many stories online, and there are several blogs that give away secrets to their success.

Read from there and increase your knowledge base on the subject. You will have the chance to interact with someone who knows what works and that will boost your confidence.

## Test

Always test out your videos on an audience before you decide to go live. You have to get an honest opinion out of people in order to know how good your stuff is. Remember to test it out on a wide range of audiences and don't stick to any one group or groups. Once you have their opinions, look for the positives and build on them and look at the negatives to reduce them. But don't ask someone who is looking to please you as they will not give you an honest opinion. Look for someone who will give you an unbiased opinion and let you know if what you have is good or not.

## Collaborate

You can choose to collaborate with someone right from the beginning. Ideally, two people who have a lot of unique subscribers collaborate, but if you think you can pay someone a little to collaborate with them and get subscribers, then you can do that. But remember, you need to have stuff that is good enough and has gone unnoticed in order for this to work.

## Reset goals

Remember to reset your goals from time to time. You have to aim high and not get stuck in the same place. Only if you aim big will you have the chance to make it big. Once you attain your goal, go for the next big thing and so on. Ultimately, you will have the opportunity to realize all your dreams and make a passive income out of YouTube.

## Take it slow

Don't rush into too many things at once. You have to take it slow and steady. This is especially important if you are restarting after a failure. Rushing will only cause further disappointment, which is not ideal. So, take it slow and make sure you are doing everything right this time around.

## Attempt Blogging

If your attempts at promoting your YouTube channel and videos fail via social media like Facebook, Twitter, and Google Plus, try starting a blog with contents related to the videos you have posted. It was mentioned previously to start a blog, but if you do not have one yet, it may be time to try creating one. You can link your channel in your blogs and vice-versa to ensure you get maximum views of both your videos as well as your blog. Commenting on other blogs with related content and linking to your videos can do wonders as you get the attention of the other blogger's followers. Make sure to never trouble the other bloggers by consistently linking your channel and videos in their blogs.

## Positivity

Remember to always remain positive. It can be a little disheartening to see others excel while you can't. But don't allow it to get to you. You have to remain positive and not give up on your endeavors.

These are the things that you can do if you are not experiencing any positive growth with your YouTube endeavors.

## Key Highlights

The very first thing to understand is the power of the Internet. It was just two decades ago when people started to discover its wonders, and now, very life depends on it. It is not possible to lead a smooth day-to-day life without having a good Internet connection. Imagine what would happen if there were none; well, we wouldn't even be having this conversation right now. So, it is vital to understand and embrace the Internet in order to find the best passive income avenues in the world. If you choose not to embrace it, then you will be left behind, and everybody will move forward towards a brighter future.

The Internet is a vast space, and there are so many things in it. From these things, you have to find the best things that will help you increase your profits. One such aspect is YouTube. YouTube is a video site that allows you to upload and download videos and watch whatever you want to. The power is in the hands of the common man, and they are allowed to add in any type of video that they like. If others like what they put up, then there is a chance for them to make money out of it.

In order to earn money, the person has to amass a certain number of people, who will regularly look at whatever is being uploaded by the person. They are known as subscribers. Once a minimum number of subscribers are attained, the person can tie up with companies who will play their ads before the person's video starts. The idea is for people to watch the video, get acquainted with the product, and buy it. But that is none of the uploader's concern. All that he or she should care about is the money that they make every time someone watches the ad.

There is no restriction on what can be taped and uploaded. However, there are some restrictions in terms of copyrights and taking content from other people's videos. There are a million ideas for videos that you can upload. We discussed some of the ideas in this book, but there are hundreds of ideas out there. You must look them up and choose the ones that are best for you. It is key to not steal anything and use other's content with due written permission. It is important for people to not copy anything as it will defeat the purpose of being unique and garnering an audience for your work. So, the key is to come up with interesting videos that will keep the audience engaged and not make them want to leave your channel.

Remember that the Internet is a very powerful tool, and you have the chance to use it to your advantage. So, if you want to raise your voice against something, then there is nothing like starting a video revolution. Videotape your protest and upload it. You will have a lot of subscribers who will gladly embed your video. You will get a lot of publicity for your videos and have the chance to make them popular. You can actually make your living out of doing this, given you get everything right. There are people out there who have quit their day jobs just by making money from YouTube.

Remember that your audience is the most vital part of your business. You have to please them and do whatever they ask of you to in order to keep them hooked. It is vital to keep in touch with them and speak with them in the comments section. It is best for the conversations to be two-way, and you must try your best to reply to all those that are loyal subscribers to your channel. Of course, you cannot talk to them all and should especially not address those that are trying to piss you off by adding in mean comments.

It is possible for you to promote your business by using YouTube. Videos are one of the most preferred ways to convey a message to a person. You can take advantage of this fact and promote your business. Make a video promoting your business or tape how to use something that your company makes. This can be a product or a service demonstration. Your video will help promote your business in a big way and garner a bigger audience. As was said before, if you don't embrace the Internet, then you will be left behind, and how!

If you have a lot of videos to offer, then you have to arrange them and try and promote the best ones. You can link everything to increase your chance of getting noticed by others. Remember that you cannot have only one video and must keep the videos coming. Do more of your popular videos and link them to older ones. You will have the chance to show your new audience what you are made of.

Collaborations are a great way to increase your business. But you need to collaborate with good YouTubers who have a large subscriber base. You can easily swap your audiences and, if you are just starting out, then garner a large audience base. If you wish to diversify what you have, then collaborate with someone who has different content, and if you wish to play it safe, then collaborate with others who have similar content as you.

We looked at AdSense in detail and answered FAQs on the topic. Hope you understood how it works and use it to your advantage.

*Andrew Mckinnon*

# Chapter 12
# YouTube Integration with Other Business Websites

In today's world, every single organization has its own assets that can be in the form of products, goods, offers, or services. The challenge lies in how the organization enables its customers to access this wide range of services to help the customers to manage them better. In this regard, YouTube is one of the best methods which provides video streaming capabilities by integrating within the organization's website. In this chapter, we will discuss various testing scenarios that will often be useful in situations where websites try to integrate with the giant YouTube.

If any organization wants to reach out to a large audience or to potential customers, they can integrate their business website with YouTube. But it is not as simple as it may appear to be. You have to take into consideration many factors, such as what scenarios will be generated when you integrate your website with the biggest video social media, YouTube.

## Testing Scenarios for YouTube Integration with other Websites:

In today's world, almost all websites present on the Internet use media campaigns in order to advertise their products. Websites often try to fit in videos on their websites for easy viewing. YouTube is the best communication medium in order to advertise services.

It is very important to know exactly what this means in the way of business generation before a website tries to integrate with YouTube, keeping in mind the testing point of view. In this chapter, we will discuss all the common testable scenarios when YouTube is integrated with any other website.

So, let us see these scenarios in detail:

Managing the Videos Scenario, basically Admin Activities:

This deals with the most basic and important activities of managing the videos. These activities are mainly carried out by the website administrator. In some scenarios, these activities are performed by other users as well, depending on how the company has set it up. It involves not only the addition of content to the video site, but it also involves modification and deletion, as these are the initial activities. So, all of this has to be taken care by the website administrator on a regular basis.

- He has capabilities to add video content from the organization's website.

- He has the ability to remove video content from the organization's website.

- He has the ability to deliver and distribute video content from the organization's website.

- He has the ability to modify video content from the organization's website.

## Video Streaming Script Scenario:

Sites provide links to videos that will be available via streaming video services. These services are important because they are at the front end of the customer experience, and the user will watch (play / pause / stop) videos via streaming video services. It should provide the user with ease of accessibility in the form of the display of the video link / icon, and the user should have the ability to play / pause / stop easily. It can be frustrating to a customer not to have these controls. It should be very easy to use and should not be too complex, so the best way is to keep it very simple at the front end. The scenarios will be generally reusable video streaming having following features:

• Capacity to watch video content on the organization's website.

• Ability to pause the video content on the organization's website.

• Capacity to fast forward the video content on the organization's website.

• Capabilities to rewind video content on the organization's website.

## Content and Ads Checking Scenario:

Content and ads management is a scenario where we need to check if the content which is available on the website is correct or not and whether it stays relevant to needs. The ads videos displayed should be short, informative, and eye catching to viewers. They should not be too long as the viewer is unlikely to stick with it if the ads overrun, and this will not work in the company's favor. As per content and ads management, you also need to check various types of statistics such as the total number of users who are viewing the content, total number of users who are visiting the site, total number of unique visits onto the site, who and what kind of users are viewing the content, and also if it controls any third party ads that are served to the customers on your website. The following main scenarios can be covered under this section:

• Capabilities to control content like who views the channel from the organization's website.

• Capabilities to control content like any third-party ads that are served to customers from the organization's website.

## Reporting and Measurements Scenario:

Reporting and Measurements is the functionality that displays the statistics related to time factors. It is important that you should know the details such as the total time length the video was used for. This includes being able to register the time when it started, the time at which it was played ¼ way through, halfway through, ¾ of the way through, and fully as well as the number of times it was replayed. By using these statistics, you can analyze customer response to the video. For example, if a video is stopped many times at a ¼ of the way through, this means it is not effective and admin can take the appropriate action like adding new content, modifying content, or removing the content to try and pull in more customers. Hence these statistics are crucial. So, an admin team needs to know this information to see how effective the video is. The following main scenarios can be covered under this section:

Capability to view and download the following metrics:

- How many times the video is displayed.

- How many times the video is played (started).

- How many times the video is played to 50%.

- How many times the video is played to 100%.

- How many times the video is replayed within same session.

## Brand Display Checking Scenario:

Every organization has a unique brand and logo. The brand suggests the organization has complete authority of the videos that are being uploaded onto its website, and customers seeing the brand can assume the videos are genuine. Organization websites should be able to display the brand properly to the customers and Internet users. If the organizations are not able to do this, then the viewers might think the video is only loosely connected to the brand. The logo should be positioned clearly enough for customers to have a distinct view on the website. It should be large enough to be noticed. Also, it should be at a distinct place in the video. Do not put it in the center of the video as it will distract the viewer while watching the video. Try to keep it at the top left or at the bottom right of the video. The following scenarios can be covered under this section:

• Capabilities to display an "on brand" channel for customers from the organization website.

• Capabilities to display an "on brand" channel for Internet users from the organization website.

## Navigation Bar Scenario:

The navigation bar is a tool which the user uses to perform the intended action when on the website. Hence, the navigation bar should satisfy entire end user requirements. The better the navigation bar options are, the better the user can access the applications with ease. Users tend to drag the cursors towards the right or left, and the video should play accordingly. It should be very smooth and should not hang up the video for long. The drag movements should be in sync with audio and video. This synchronization is central to user experience. If there is any time lag, then this will detract from the user experience, and they are unlikely to watch the whole video.

Upon finishing on the video content, the cursor position should move to the initial position, and the user should have an option to play the video again if that is their wish. The following main scenarios can be covered under this section:

Scenarios related to verification of navigation bar following capabilities:

• Dragging left to right and checking time variance accordingly.

• Dragging right to left and checking time variance accordingly.

• Once video is finished, navigation bar should move to initial position.

The last point is particularly relevant because it gives the user the chance to re-watch the video if they were experiencing difficulties because of a bad Internet connection.

## Audio and Video Sync Scenario:

In a case where the integration between the website and YouTube is not 100% in sync, then the synchronization between audio and video during runtime will cause issues to arise, which make the video difficult to watch. Hence, from a testing prospective, you should make sure that the sync is as near to 100 % as possible. In fact, this is one of the most important scenarios to be tested before the start of actual testing of efficiency and gathering of statistics. If the synchronization between audio and video is not perfect, then it will be a complete waste of the video, and no one will watch it because viewers like to watch a video that has perfect synchronization of video and audio. The following main scenarios can be covered under this section:

• Check the synchronization between audio and video during runtime.

## Audio-Related Scenarios:

These are general audio-related scenarios that are mainly involved in verification of the various functionalities of the audio. It includes how advertisements are getting loaded, loading time, delays, audio quality verification, correct and accurate audio, mute buttons functionalities, etc. Supposing a video is muted at a particular moment, then the mute should be instant. There should not be any delay between pressing mute and the sound stopping. A delay of even one second can cause user annoyance. The following main scenarios can be covered under this section:

Scenarios that verify the audio-related properties:

- How many times the advertisements are loading.

- Audio quality verification.

- Correct audio verification.

- Mute verification.

- Verification of audio on expand and collapse of an expandable advertisement.

## Video-Related Scenarios:

These are general video-related scenarios that mainly involve verification of the video. It includes cases like how the advertisements are getting loaded, loading time, delays, video quality verification, correct and accurate video rendition, mute button response, auto play verification, etc. The following main scenarios can be covered under this section:

Scenarios that verify the video-related properties:

- Advertisements loading.

- Video quality verification.

- Correct video verification.

- Video controls verification.

- Verification of audio on expand and collapse of an expandable advertisement.

- Auto-play verification scenario.

## Negative/Erroneous Scenarios:

These are scenarios that are aimed at showing the software does not work correctly. It is also known as "test to fail." Negative scenarios ensure that your application can handle invalid input or unexpected user behavior. The video should be able to take care of these issues and should not rely upon the browser to take care of them.

The following can be negative scenarios in the case of video streaming functionality:

- No audio.

- No video.

- Plays with sound but no vision.

- Plays with vision but no sound.

- Errors related to "unable to download codec."

- Page not displayed related errors.

*Andrew Mckinnon*

# Chapter 13
# Customizing MySpace and YouTube Brand Channel

## YouTube Channels:

The YouTube channel page holds the information of the user visiting it. All the registered users of YouTube will have a normal channel page. In the channel pages, all the videos that are marked by the user as his favorites can be viewed and also the individual playlist can be displayed. The normal channel page can be changed to a brand channel if the user meets the requirement of having a self-created video. Thus, a normal user will have access to an area that only allows adding videos to his favorite list.

## Channel Page layout:

The layout includes the following content areas.

1.     The channel banner which measures 960 pixel by 150 pixel and appears at the top of the page.

2.     The video navigator of 960 pixel by 670 pixel that allows users to watch the uploaded videos and playlists.

3.     Channel ID module that helps the YouTube user to interact with the channel. This module has the name of the channel and the link for subscribing to the channel.

4.     Channel information module that describes the channel and includes the profile and the honors section.

5.     Side column image for linking to the external websites or to external YouTube links.

6.     Ad module that is present in the top right area of the page.

## Customizing the Brand Channel page:

The YouTube Brand Channel offers a layout adjustment facility. To customize the account the following steps are to be followed,

1.    Login to the YouTube account.

2.    Click the username.

3.    Click on my channel option.

4.    Click the channel settings button.

The brand channel page has three tabs for customizing the channel's content which include appearance, info and settings, and Featured Tab.

## Appearance tab

The appearance tab allows the user to update the images for the channel page. The user avatar (of a size up to 1600 X 1600 pixels) can be updated in the appearance tab. Image types can be .JPG, .GIF, .BMP, or .PNG. This gives the option to choose the channel's background image and also to select whether or not to repeat the background, and there is a fill color option for filling in the background. The image will appear centered on the channel.

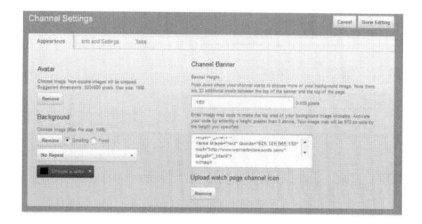

The channel banner is uploaded in the appearance tab. On entering a value of 150 pixels, the modules in the channel page will be pushed down, and the custom HTML box will appear on the page. If the height is not specified, the banner will remain hidden. The banners cannot exceed 970 pixels by 150 pixels, and the file size should be less than 256k.

## Image Map:

The <map> tag, which is a client-side image-map, is used for placing the channel banner content. Image map refers to the clickable areas in an image. The map tag uses the

<area> tag that specifies the area in the image map. The cords attribute of the <area> tag specifies the coordinates of the area. The different types of coords are:

Rect – A four sided figure.

Circle – A circle.

Polygon – Multisided figure.

Rect attribute is used for image mapping in YouTube pages. The href attribute of the <area> tag determines the hyperlink target for the area.

A sample image map for the channel banner:

<map name="new_page_image_map">

<area shape= "rect" cords="0, 0,870,180" href="/" target="_blank">

</map>

## Info and Settings tab:

This tab lets the user customize the channel's title, description, and the tags. The character count of the description filed is about 1,000 characters, 255 characters of which will be displayed in the "about" section of the channel. On tagging the page, it will get listed in the search results when a user searches for the tag.

## Featured Tab:

This tab provides the option to organize and display the videos. Three templates are provided by default for organizing the contents that includes overview, blogger, and everything.

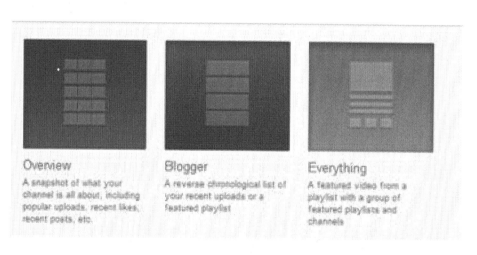

The featured tab has a featured video player that indicates the type of channel to the user. On clicking each of the tabs, the preview of the channel will be updated with the respective template. After customizing all the options, the

"Done editing" has to be clicked for the changes to get reflected on the page.

## Watch Page Customization:

Watch page is a page where the user can view the video and all the information about the video.

The watch page channel icon is a 25-pixel image. It appears in the video watch page above the video player and is linked to the channel page. The watch page channel icon has to be updated in the appearance tab in the channel-editing interface.

For customizing the watch page the following steps have to be followed.

1.    Click on the user name.

2.    Go to settings.

3.    The user profile can be updated in the overview link of the account settings tab.

4.    The sharing link helps in sharing the activity of the user to social networking sites like Facebook and Twitter.

5.  In the account-setting tab, click the watch branding for customizing the watch page.

The background image of 1200 pixels by 628 pixels can be uploaded for the watch page. The background color and the text color can be selected. The banner and the corresponding links can be updated in the options provided. The small banner must be 670 pixels by 70 pixels high and will be applied for the small player while the large banner is of 854 pixels by 70 pixels high and will be applied for the large player. Mobile banner and the playlist to display can also be updated.

Image map for small banner:

<map name=" new_page_small_banner_image_map">

<area shape= "rect" cords="0, 0, 760,670" href="/" target="_blank">

</map>

Image map for large banner:

<map name=" new_page_large_banner_image_map ">

```
<area shape= "rect" cords="0, 0, 684, 60" href="/"
target="_blank">
```

```
</map>
```

The watch branding page:

## MySpace customization:

MySpace is a popular social networking site. MySpace has premade backgrounds. For customizing these, the following steps have to be followed.

1.    Log into the MySpace profile.

2.    Click the "customize" link present on the page.

3.    The "look and feel" option helps the user change the theme of the page with predefined themes.

4.    The "modules and marquee" allows the user to update the modules and also to add a marquee that increases the space between the header and the content. The marquee can be 250 pixels in height to fit it to the page. The links for banners can be updated to the marquee.

5.    Browse the different themes available, and, after verifying the look and feel of the page, the settings can be saved. The new theme will be applied on the profile page.

MySpace has the option for adding a custom CSS theme. The tool name "Theme Machine" is used for custom themes. Go to http://www.myspace.com/thememachine

and accept the terms and conditions for using the custom theme.

The advanced options include the following fields for customization:

Base styles: The background image and the fill color along with the font color and type can be updated here.

User navigation: Lets the user update the navigation bar that is present in the left column of the page. The normal and the hover color can be updated.

Status heading, user heading, profile modules, tabs, and paginations: These options let the user style the corresponding sections.

Content wrap: Allows the user to select the inner or outer wrap. The Outer wrap wraps the entire content and provides the background color unlike the inner wrap that does not enclose the modules in a wrapper.

Custom CSS: CSS styles can be added through this option.

# Conclusion

Thank you for choosing this book. I hope you found it informative and easy to comprehend.

YouTube is there for you to use and make the most of it. Don't worry about any competition that is out there and concentrate only on your own channel. If you have a fixed mindset, then you will never make it big. You have to therefore have a "growth" mindset in order to increase your growth. If you think you are happy having only a few thousand subscribers, then you will never make it big. You have to aim higher and keep going upward.

I'm sure you now have a pretty good idea about YouTube and more specifically on how you can utilize this platform to your benefit. Using this amazing social media platform is fairly easy, and the right effort can help you earn some good money through it. Try out the guidelines in this book and see how it works for you. You can keep at it and make your channel a bigger success with time. You have to look at the positives and the negatives and do whatever is best for you. Don't copy someone else's strategy as what is working for them might not work for you. So, be unique and forge ahead.

Don't be disappointed if you are not able to make a lot of money initially. Profit from passive income is always cumulative, and there will be a time when you will be thoroughly satisfied with the amount of money that you make from it. Until such time, you have to stay put and pursue your online business.

If you think any of your friends and family can benefit from the content in this book, you can even go ahead and recommend it. As for yourself, keep referring back to this book if you need some pointers while you set up your income generating YouTube channel as well.